MAGNETIC
MARKETING

FOR DENTISTS

MAGNETIC MARKETING

FOR DENTISTS

HOW TO ATTRACT A FLOOD OF NEW PATIENTS
THAT **PAY, STAY,** AND **REFER**

DAN S. KENNEDY

WITH THE **MAGNETIC MARKETING** TEAM

ForbesBooks

Published by ForbesBooks, Charleston, South Carolina.
Member of Advantage Media Group.

ForbesBooks is a registered trademark, and the ForbesBooks colophon is a trademark of Forbes Media, LLC.

Printed in the United States of America.

10 9 8 7 6 5 4 3 2 1

ISBN: 978-1-950863-69-3
LCCN: 2020917167

This custom publication is intended to provide accurate information and the opinions of the author in regard to the subject matter covered. It is sold with the understanding that the publisher, Advantage|ForbesBooks, is not engaged in rendering legal, financial, or professional services of any kind. If legal advice or other expert assistance is required, the reader is advised to seek the services of a competent professional.

Advantage Media Group is proud to be a part of the Tree Neutral® program. Tree Neutral offsets the number of trees consumed in the production and printing of this book by taking proactive steps such as planting trees in direct proportion to the number of trees used to print books. To learn more about Tree Neutral, please visit www.treeneutral.com.

Since 1917, Forbes has remained steadfast in its mission to serve as the defining voice of entrepreneurial capitalism. ForbesBooks, launched in 2016 through a partnership with Advantage Media Group, furthers that aim by helping business and thought leaders bring their stories, passion, and knowledge to the forefront in custom books. Opinions expressed by ForbesBooks authors are their own. To be considered for publication, please visit www.forbesbooks.com.

Contents

BUILDING YOUR MAGNETIC MARKETING® SYSTEM

Learn the Secrets of the Most Successful Dentists Who Have Created a Flood of New Patients

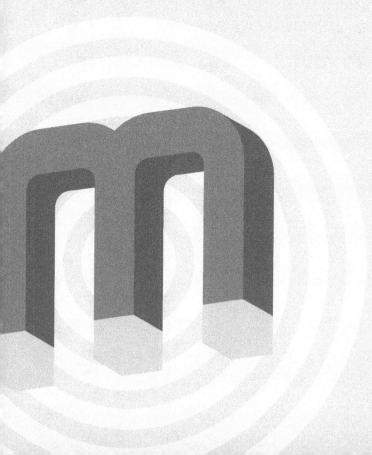

You have finally found it!

The one place created for dentists seeking to finally answer that common, nagging question:

"Why am I working harder, but not seeing more money?"

All dentists, regardless of their current success or lack of success, are stuck—either you're growing or you're dying. There is no middle ground. Which leaves you with great opportunity.

You have worked hard, created a good practice with steady revenue, a somewhat reliable patient base, and profit margins that at least keep you above water.

Yet you feel like the proverbial hamster on the wheel. You keep running faster and faster, and yet you can't seem to break that cycle. Every day feels like a struggle just to keep your head above water. You're wondering what happened to that dream of owning a thriving practice—a dream where you didn't have to worry about money, where you could take an afternoon off, carefree, to watch your child's school play. What happened to that dream?

You've tried marketing: you've spent serious money on ads that didn't work, direct mail that underdelivered, pay-per-click advertising that drained your bank account dry, and probably a host of other approaches, none of which delivered the results promised or expected.

Like most dentists who own their practice, you sometimes feel confused and overwhelmed: getting hammered on all sides with "consultants" saying do one thing or another, after another, and feeling like you have to press harder, to do more and more—just to get the same results. Or less.

I'm here to help you—to mute all that noise and provide you with a set of principles (not tactics) and the resources to magnetically attract patients who are ready, willing, and able to move forward with you.

And by resources, I mean my duplicatable machine for not only attracting patients, but converting leads into patients and multiplying one patient into two.

Marketing is an ever-changing world, as new media seems to pop up every day, but if you learn the principles that allow you to magnetically attract patients, you can make any media, at any time, work. When you develop a system that feeds you new patients on a daily basis, you will never feel the anxiety of wondering when or where your next patient will come from! In fact, you can finally take a vacation without checking your phone every hour.

If you're at least open to the notion that maybe, just maybe, there's a better way forward than the one you've traveled thus far— and if you're reading this now with an open mind willing to cautiously believe in that possibility...

Then this book is for you.

WHY I WROTE THIS BOOK

I'm here to offer a radical and challenging idea that just about everything you think you know and have been conditioned to believe about growing your dental practice is wrong.

I am here to mute the noise and guide you to clarity about a relatively short list of fundamental principles and strategies that can prevent you from being lost in a dense forest of media demanding your attention, time, and money.

> **Everything you think you know and have been conditioned to believe about growing your dental practice is wrong.**

If you get it, you'll smack yourself in the head for not seeing it all sooner on your own. You'll be in awe of how much sense it makes. You'll never look at an ad, sales letter, or website the same again. Traditional advertising and marketing will be ruined for you.

But let me warn you: when you do get it, you'll be criticized by team members, argued with by everyone, ridiculed by even family and friends. You will need your results and a steel spine to stay strong. The outstanding results you'll see when shifting from ordinary marketing to response-driven marketing will convince you. You will need courage and discipline to stay your new course.

I promise you that being thought a "fool" or "misguided renegade" and having millions of dollars trumps being thought of as "normal" and "correct" and "proper" and barely making a living.

WHERE DID THESE IDEAS ORIGINATE?

These ideas began with a discovery—or more accurately, a series of discoveries—that could well form the most important realization you ever arrive at as a businessperson. It's disappointing and frustrating at first, but empowering if embraced and acted upon.

I discovered:

→ You can have the most wonderful dental practice imaginable, offering the best service ever, and still starve.

→ You can be a spectacular sales person and still starve.

→ You can have a positive attitude that Norman Vincent Peale would envy, and be as motivated as a participant at a Tony Robbins seminar, and still starve.

→ You can be a master closer, selling your services at will, left and right, and still starve.

→ You can provide great value, great service, great expertise, and still starve.

→ Your dental practice can literally be a paragon of virtues, with the world seemingly singing your praises twenty-four seven, and even as you bask in their applause, you can still starve.

The realization that you must come to is this: you could very well starve, you won't get rich, and you certainly won't have peace of mind…

Unless and until you have an affordable, efficient, dependable means of attracting a sufficient flow of qualified LEADS and PATIENTS.

Most dentists sort of know this, but they still focus on everything but the one thing that will make all the difference in the world to their success: *Marketing.*

All the frustrations and internal problems you're experiencing with your practice today are because you DON'T have a good Marketing *System.*

Many practices offer great services, quality care, incredible patient experience—all that and more—but they fail because they can't give themselves enough new sales opportunities. To paraphrase Thoreau, most dentists lead lives of desperation because they don't know how to create a steady and sufficient supply of qualified patients.

> **To paraphrase Thoreau, most dentists lead lives of desperation because they don't know how to create a steady and sufficient supply of qualified patients.**

IT'S TIME FOR A DIFFERENT VISION

I've been teaching these principles in various forms since the mid-1970s; due to the dire economic conditions at that time, I referred to them as "The Small Business Emergency Survival Kit." They have gradually grown into the system I call Magnetic Marketing today, which has spread throughout the United States and indeed all over the world.

The principles in this book have been tested over and over again, not just by myself, but by entrepreneurs and business owners of all shapes, sizes, locations, and industries. Today, we have students in sixty-seven different countries using these principles to create a steady flow of new customers, clients, or patients in their businesses. They use these strategies to scale, grow, and differentiate their businesses—to rise above price competition and to quickly demand (and receive) top dollar for their services.

As you read through this book, you may feel as if you have heard pieces of this before. I hope you have. I have been sharing these principles since the 1970s. Hundreds of thousands heard my message when I was on the SUCCESS Tour, have purchased my training programs, have participated in my coaching groups, or have been private clients. Thanks to Magnetic Marketing, this message, these principles, and their influence continue to grow. There are many out there teaching these ideas. Some give me credit; some don't.

Today, you are hearing the entire story straight from the horse's mouth.

Today, I am here to give you the entire vision plus the architecture that will allow you to make this vision a reality.

The vision of being the prosperous owner of a dental practice that's a *REAL* business—not of random or episodic income events, not of endless need for the next new promotion, not of frequent worry where the next appointment or procedure might come from.

The vision of certainty and security and stability. Of a continuous and steady inflow of desired patients who trust you, rely on you, and refer their friends and family to you. Even of creating equity and wealth, not just day-to-day income.

The vision is based on two specific promises I'll make concerning what you'll discover as you go through this book:

1. I promise to take you beyond just another trick or two that might produce a bump in website conversions temporarily, or a social media hack that everybody is excited about momentarily, and instead show you a *SYSTEM* for marketing that you can quickly begin using to make significantly more money across *ALL* your communication channels and media choices.

2. In this book I will reveal the powerful, proven secrets to attracting opportunity into your practice, acquiring an abundance of high-quality patients, and creating a sustainable practice. You'll realize what you must build for yourself to create true freedom, stability, and scalability.

You do *NOT* need any special background, education, or skills to use this – other than a commitment to use it. You can apply it to any kind of practice serving any kind of market. I have students using what I'll share here with dental practices of all shapes, sizes, and market demographics. You'll meet doctors later who'll demonstrate exactly how this *SYSTEM* works for them.

For now, know that YOU CAN turbocharge your ability to magnetically attract and achieve with what you'll discover in the following pages.

Let's begin.

P.S. You do NOT need to read this entire book before also taking some next steps to connect with me and with Magnetic Marketing. Feel free to take advantage of the invitations on the next page NOW.

Visit us online to access these valuable resources.

Where Should I Start?

The most common question we get from Dan Kennedy book readers and entrepreneurs who find us after hearing about Magnetic Marketing is…"Where Should I Start?" Dan Kennedy has been at this for over 40 years and has a vault of content that's the size of a small bank, not the vault in a bank, but enough content to fill a small bank. The quick two question survey will provide you a simple road map to success **whether you're finding us for the first time, or you are an advanced student** of Magnetic Marketing and Dan Kennedy.

→ Get Started at
   MagneticMarketing.com/get-started-dental

How Magnetic is Your Marketing Today?

One reason so many practice owners become advertising victims is because they don't understand the foundation of the Magnetic Marketing system. **For a limited time, we're offering a complimentary "How Magnetic Is Your Business & Your Marketing Assessment" to listeners and readers of Magnetic Marketing.** Record your answers to 8 short questions to find out how magnetically attractive you currently are. Your answers will unlock access to your personalized roadmap for your practice.

→ Complete your Assessment at **MagneticMarketing.com/magnetic-practice**

60-Day Test Drive of Magnetic Marketing Gold Membership

Get **Instant Access** to Dan Kennedy's Magnetic Marketing System (what this entire book is about!) and **A 60 Day Trial** of the No B.S. Magnetic Marketing Newsletter for just 2 easy payments of just

$59.97. Plus, if you take us up on this VERY Special, Limited Time Offer, you'll also receive **6 Gifts Valued At $950.85**…and even if you decide to leave our community after 60 Days, you'll keep these bonuses as our gift to you.

→ Start Your Test Drive Today at **MagneticMarketing. com/book-test-drive**

Magnetic Marketing in Action

On the Magnetic Marketing Podcast, each week we bring on members of the Magnetic Marketing community who are implementing Magnetic Marketing in their businesses and practices. Learn from the best as they share what's working, what's not working, what they have learned, and what is fueling their growth today.

→ Listen to the Latest Episodes at **MagneticMarketing.com/podcast-reader**

Take the Patient Relationship Assessment

Find out your Patient Relationship Score today!
During times of uncertainty there is ONE thing that can help your practice prosper and provide you with the stability and opportunity to grow your practice as you desire.

What is It?
A High Patient Relationship Score. There's no better way to ensure your success than to create lifelong relationships with your existing patients.

We've created a simple 9 Question Assessment that will reveal your Patient Relationship Score in under 3 minutes and share with you exactly how you can quickly improve your score.

→ Get Your Patient Relationship Score Now at **mLiveSoftware.com/assessment**

FOUNDATIONS OF MAGNETIC MARKETING

What If Everything You've Ever Been Told About Growing Your Dental Practice Was Wrong?

I am sorry to tell you that you have been lied to for a very long time!

Note that I didn't use softer words like "misled," "misinformed," or "offered less-than-optimal advice." Nope. I laid it out straight and plain.

You've been *lied to*.

It's critical to your success that I open your eyes to this fact. And I hope you're interested in the blunt, unvarnished truth about what entrepreneurial dentists actually do to create top income, wealth, independence, and sustainability. Frankly, not everyone is ready for such a conversation. Many prefer excuses to achievement. Others prefer fantasy to reality.

What I'm about to teach you will radically alter how you acquire patients and boost your revenues and profits. I have a track record of forty-five-plus years of creating multimillionaires and seven-figure-income earners. I am a made-from-scratch multimillionaire and serial entrepreneur, and I'm doing real work in the trenches right now, working with real clients and solving real issues. In fact, in one recent year alone, the combined revenues of my small cadre of private clients exceeded $1 billion.

And every marketing plan I've ever devised for any client—and they now number in the hundreds and hundreds, commanding fees exceeding $100,000, plus royalties—every one of them has been based on the *SYSTEM* I'm going to reveal in this book.

This book is for dental practice owners who see themselves not only as doctors, but as entrepreneurs. It pulls back the curtain on real-world strategies I've revealed to the thousands just like you who have subscribed to my "No B.S. Magnetic Marketing Letter," and use my systems to transform "ordinary" businesses into extraordinary money machines that far outperform their industry norms, peers, competitors and the wildest imaginations of the owners.

How do they do it?

By making the strategic switch from traditional advertising to a response-driven advertising strategy we call Magnetic Marketing.

Magnetic Marketing was created to help entrepreneurs and business owners of all kinds—with *NO* marketing knowledge or expertise—and empower them to create compelling marketing on their own without hiring outside help.

Magnetic Marketing has impacted thousands of businesses, professions, industries, and product and service categories, literally changing the way their customers, clients, and patients are obtained. (Indeed, today they form what could well be called a "secret society" of people who have figured it out.)

Its roots go back decades, if not centuries. Its core foundational principle is that every advertisement, promotion, email, flyer, TV commercial, etc., focuses *ALL* energy on:

→ identifying exactly whom you want to be your patient; and

→ getting them to respond in a specific way—not wasting any effort on branding, image, humor, style, or anything else.

THIS is the kind of marketing we'll discuss in this book—marketing designed to "magnetically attract" in a specific, repeatable, measurable way. And this is the *ONLY* model of marketing that you should model and use.

When you embrace this, you become a part of a movement that I started over two decades ago and that's now carried on by the company I founded thirty-eight years ago, Magnetic Marketing, which continues to provide powerful marketing and business growth strategies to maximize the success of entrepreneurs and practice owners all over the world—a rare feat, considering how many companies have come and gone over that period of time.

LET'S DISPEL THE MYTHS...

Personally, early on I went through a painful phase of thinking where I believed that I should be successful by my willingness to work hard and by offering products and services that were truly valuable.

As logical as this may sound, it's merely a painful myth. I still struggled.

And so I immersed myself in self-help, personal improvement, and motivational materials. I said affirmations. I thought only positive thoughts. I believed. And still I struggled—even with great products and what I believed was a great mindset to go with them.

My life only changed when it dawned on me that *great* was no better than *lousy* if I had no able, willing, ready buyers to present *great* to.

This is the key realization.

Without a sufficient and steady stream of people with whom you can exchange value for money, nothing else about your practice matters. Not your most excellent website. Not your high-visibility location. Not your credentials, degrees, certifications, education, etc. Not your hardworking, nose-to-the-grindstone ethic.

Being more talented or skilled than others in your area of dental expertise has *ZERO* value if you cannot harness the principles and power of *magnetic attraction* in a practical way.

Having the very best, most innovative, most beneficial health-care services has *ZERO* value if you cannot harness the principles and power of *magnetic attraction* in a practical way.

Many harm themselves by denying or decrying this reality. They desperately want to believe that better is better...having better credentials...having gone to a better school...having more and better experience...having more and better integrity...better work ethic, better at paying your dues...better technology and tools...etc. BETTER *SHOULD* BE ENOUGH.

Maybe in an idyllic and just world that would be so.

But not in *THIS* world.

In this world, you are not automatically awarded what you deserve or think you deserve. It's not a pure meritocracy. If that were the case, there'd probably be no rich porn stars and no poor pastors and preachers. I have learned and taught that money moves about for its own reasons, and neither need nor deservingness are magnetic to it.

It depends on powerful, well-crafted, measurable strategies—a tried-and-true system—rooted in common sense that work across all kinds of media. The strategies that we'll talk about have been applied in 136 different business categories by over 93,417 entrepreneurs in sixty-seven different countries: *they deliver.*

In other words, Magnetic Marketing is as proven as the law of gravity, and as a law, much like gravity is, you cannot fix it; you can only know it and change your actions to fit into the section you want to. I tell you this because it may require some patience from you for you to really get it and use it, but like gravity, you cannot defy its facts.

This switch is critical because…

YOU'VE BEEN SET UP TO *FAIL*

If you've managed to survive as a dentist even a year or two in business, it's obvious that you've gone well beyond the limited framework provided by our "educational system" when it comes to grasping the core principles of marketing.

But even with the scant marketing education your peers in dentistry may have acquired from school, mentors, and self-schooling, the fact is that most of them are like the blind leading the blind. Even the highly vaunted MBA accreditations typically fail to deliver serious, real-world, bottom-line results when put to the test of facing the dog-eat-dog frenzy of the marketplace.

I set before you as proof the financial reality that in every profession, every category of business, every sales team, every population, these figures hold true:

→ One percent create tremendous incomes and wealth.

→ Four percent do very well.

→ Fifteen percent earn good livings.

→ Sixty percent struggle endlessly.

→ Twenty percent fail.

In a nutshell, 80 percent do poorly, and 20 percent succeed.

Why, then, would you want to copy the marketing done by the majority when facts show it *FAILS THEM*? Why should you follow that same path to frustration and failure?

Most "ordinary" businesses believe they have to advertise and market like much bigger brand-name companies, so they invest (waste) lots of money in many different kinds of media to promote image, brand, and presence.

You *CANNOT* make the mistake of jumping into media because "everyone else is using it." Big-name brands have all sorts of reasons for the way they advertise and market that have ZERO to do with getting a patient or selling treatment plans. Your agenda is much simpler; in fact, there's a huge difference between how BIG corporations consider marketing and how you as an entrepreneurial dentist see it:

Big Corporation Agenda for Advertising and Marketing

→ Please/appease its board of directors (most of whom know zip about advertising and marketing but have lots of opinions)

→ Please/appease its stockholders.

→ Look good and appropriate to Wall Street.

→ Look good and appropriate to the media.

→ Build brand identity.

→ Win awards for advertising.

→ Sell something.

YOUR Agenda

→ Sell something. NOW!

I realized a long time ago that big, dumb corporations were using sloppy, wasteful mass-advertising practices that had them hemorrhaging money left and right.

But that didn't stop dentists of all kinds from modeling what they saw, read, and heard every day, wrongly thinking that "if it works for them, it's gotta work for us too."

Here's the No BS Truth: The typical dentist is essentially clueless when it comes to advertising and marketing. This makes them highly vulnerable to becoming what I call "Advertising Victims": easy prey for media salespeople and ad agencies and anyone else who doesn't know how to actually close the deal and make a sale.

Think I'm wrong?

If you ever manage to corner one of your peers, try to get him to tell you with confidence *WHERE* his patients and treatment plan sales come from, what it costs to get a patient, what kind of results one ad gets versus another. Try. He can't. He's guessing. And that's what the industry vultures rely on: they know that when their client (i.e., *YOU*) can only guess how well their marketing works, they have a credit card they can ding regularly and without fail.

I realized something different had to be done, because you need a saner, more productive path to growth that makes your life more pleasant, lucrative, and certain.

AND IT'S NOT ABOUT WORKING HARDER

You've been told, over and over again, the answer to all your troubles is to:

→ Work Harder

→ Work Smarter

→ Work Harder and Smarter

Sorry, but none of those will fly or even come close to hitting the mark.

It's not about working harder and being smarter about how you do so. I'm willing to wager you've already gone down that road and have done all you can do and the results just weren't there.

You don't need more hard work...not from yourself, your spouse, your team—nobody. Instead, you need a NEW strategy. You need a SYSTEM—one that works for you, 24/7/365, doing all this for you:

→ Generates a predictable flow of
  new patients to your doorstep

→ Turns every patient into two patients

→ Creates repeatable appointments and business

→ Allows you freedom (financial and time)

→ Focuses on marketing

The more productive answer is to develop a SYSTEM that attracts new patients to you in an organized way.

WHY NOW IS THE RIGHT TIME
FOR THIS NEW SYSTEM

The system I'm about to reveal to you in this book will radically change your thinking about what you invest your time in, what's truly important when it comes to making money, and the way you communicate your ideas, services, and worth to the world.

It's a much more sophisticated way of creating power for yourself in a cluttered marketplace, *a systematic way to magnetically attract your ideal patients to your practice.*

It is a system that gives you reliable and predictable results so you finally know that when you invest X dollars, you can expect Y number of leads, then Z number of appointments or selling opportunities.

You want a system that enables you to better target the most appropriate and valuable patients for your practice so you're not wasting time, energy, resources scurrying down rabbit holes chasing "would-be" patients who in fact will "never-be."

Most importantly, you need a system you can comprehend and control.

It's just too complicated to wing it on your own anymore. Way back when, I managed my own mailings with a printout of the prospect list, a stack of envelopes, and an occasionally amenable cat to lick the stamps. It worked great for me then, but today's barrage of media options makes such a simple operation not only outdated but also terribly self-limiting. Media choices abound, and multichannel marketing funnels that best leverage the unique strengths of each is the proper path. You can't succeed with a haphazard approach.

You *MUST* follow a well-conceived, testable, scalable, practical system—and you've come to the right person to reveal just such a system to you.

THEY CALL ME "THE PROFESSOR OF HARSH REALITY"

It's a title I proudly embrace. Reality and life have always been harsh. As Hollywood legend John Wayne once said:

"Life is hard. And it's harder if you're stupid."

In forty-five years of helping all kinds of entrepreneurs and businesses achieve their dreams, I've realized that business owners aren't actually "stupid" when it comes to raw cerebral horsepower. The problem lies in the "stupid" things they do that they've been led to believe are true.

That may seem a bit blunt, or even a bit uncomfortable. Good.

I unapologetically wrote this book to offer the blunt, unvarnished truth about how dentists really CAN create a flood of new patients while building wealth, independence, and sustainability.

There are a lot of numbers bandied about in marketing: response percentages, circulation, pass-along effect, visitors, dedicated visitors, likes, friends, fans, and on and on. I'm here to tell you it's all BS. It's all about leads that convert to income. Period.

And the very worst number in business is *ONE*. If you are overly dependent on any *ONE* thing in your business, you will at some point be punished for this vulnerability. You can bank on that. One key team member, one key account or patient, one service, one skill, one technology—all woefully insecure and unstable. This is particularly true of MEDIA.

It's about attracting more patients who respect and value what you do so much so that they are willing to pay for it. It's not about just bringing in more (quantity); it's about bringing in more of the right people (quality).

And the foundational key to making this happen…

YOU *MUST* SEPARATE YOURSELF FROM THE COMPETITION

I want you to understand that whatever your deliverables are, they are not your dental practice.

You must make yourself the go-to person, place, or entity for some audience that can be interested in you and your deliverables. And the primary way to accomplish this is by crafting an answer to this question:

"Why should I choose you versus any and every other option of the same dental product or service that you provide?"

Resolved with what legendary ad man Rosser Reeves called a Unique Selling Proposition (USP).

Tremendous turnarounds in business have taken place as the result of great USPs. Domino's Pizza was originally driven by a marketing message that everybody came to know: "Fresh, hot pizza delivered in thirty minutes or less, guaranteed."

If you dissect it, you'll see some interesting things. First of all, it doesn't claim to be all things to all people. There's no mention of Mama's recipe from the old country. No mention of a special sauce. In fact, there's not even any mention of *good* pizza. All it says is that it is going to get to you while it's still hot and it's still fresh and that they guarantee to do that.

What is your USP? This is going to take a little bit of work. Somewhere in your practice, there is a good answer. If not, you need to make one.

Unfortunately, the first thing one does when we start to talk about Unique Selling Proposition is to jump to the conclusion that there is nothing special about them. Sometimes in rare instances, that's true. That's when you have to do some creative thinking to make it into something unique.

Here are three questions you can ask yourself to help kick-start the process of finding or creating your USP:

Truth - Respect - Gel/If Say (t

1.   **What specifically do you do that's truly different compared to competitors?**

For Domino's, it was originally being there in thirty minutes or less. More recently, they revolutionized the company against badly sagging sales by taking the worst-ranked pizza to the best ranked for taste and quality. But that's actually the ante to already being in the game.

2.   **How do you uniquely benefit your target market?** *Ymth* *→ Indiv.*

Family

J. K. Rowling of the *Harry Potter* books and her publisher made each new book's release of exceptional benefit to independent bookstores with a devised plan for big events: books held back to release at midnight, drawing huge numbers of kids and parents into these stores, milling about at parties in costume, snacking and browsing and buying other books for an hour or more before the clock struck midnight.

The target market, the bookstore owner, was uniquely benefited in reciprocity. Rowling got far more promotional work out of the store owners than hundreds of other authors of other children's fantasy books.

3.   Can you niche your target market in a way nobody else can or will?

One of my students, a lawyer named Bill Hammond, created Alzheimer's law, a subset of elder law essentially wrapping traditional estate planning, Medicare and Medicaid planning, and other family legal matters inside a differently described package, positioned for families with a senior showing signs of or having been diagnosed with dementia. This enabled Bill to use the exact lead-generation strategies laid out in this system.

Take the time to create your own USP. It's one of the greatest marketing weapons you can ever have for your practice.

CHAPTER 2

Why Marketing Fails

Over the course of this book, you're going to discover a totally new and different way to market your practice.

In fact, you could consider this "an alternate universe" of marketing, where all the fundamentals you thought were true have been turned on their head. Kind of like that episode in *Star Trek* where Captain Kirk was a bad guy and Spock sported an eminently logical goatee.

It's important that you set aside any preconceptions you might have about changing gears with your marketing, because the fact of the matter is clear and has been for years. Indeed, way back in 2006, long before the explosion of social media like Facebook, LinkedIn, Instagram, YouTube, and much more, I wrote something that remains as true today as ever, especially for dentists:

"Most advertising and marketing STINKS."

I stand by this still. Monstrous sums are wasted and opportunities lost. Even amid all the change in technology and practically limitless options available to get your message out, nothing has changed for the better. In fact, if anything, it's gotten worse.

Dentists are really confused and overwhelmed—told they must do this, that, the other thing, more and more, just to get the same results.

I'm here to guide you to clarity about a relatively short list of mistakes that, when understood and addressed, can safeguard your sanity from the assault of a thousand points of media options demanding your attention, time, and money.

MISTAKE #1: MARKETING TO THE WRONG PEOPLE

Most dentists market to the wrong people. When their marketing fails to deliver, they blame it on something else, as if it's not pretty enough, it's not big enough, we didn't get the messaging right, the billboard's stuck in the wrong location, we didn't advertise in the right magazine or on the right cable channel, or whatever.

I'm not saying that any of these factors *AREN'T* a problem. They very well could play a role in any ad's success or lack thereof.

But the bigger problem is the simple fact that in most cases, most advertising is not directed at any one person. Instead, it's directed at EVERYONE.

The marketing lacks a clear understanding of *WHOM* they are trying to target.

And here's the rub. Unless you have extremely deep pockets like one of the giant DSOs, you CAN'T market to everyone. You have to discriminate. It's not a bad word; in fact, it's your safe passage to focus and prosperity.

When you focus on a specific *WHO*, you're able to home in on exactly what makes that person tick. You're able to adjust your offers and your messaging in a way that perfectly matches their desires and abilities to fulfill those desires. Knowing that WHO inside and out enables you to craft a compelling, emotional message that reaches deep into their hopes, dreams, fears, and pain.

At any given moment in time, only 5 percent at best are intellectually, emotionally, practicably, and financially ready to act on or make any kind of decision about you or your practice. Inevitably, 95 percent of most advertising falls on deaf ears.

This makes it imperative to hit the bull's-eye with the 5 percent by narrowing your focus. However, you can and should also scheme to get those who aren't ready but will be to raise their hands early, and we'll get to this later in this book.

MISTAKE #2: SAYING THE WRONG THINGS

Not only does your marketing have to talk to the right person, it has to say the right things to that person. When you say something that fails to connect with your target patient, we call that a failed "Message to Market Match."

Going back to my example of Domino's USP, they understood their initial market perfectly: ravenously hungry college students desperate for something, anything, to ease the munchies. Their message was "fresh, hot pizza in thirty minutes or less"—the perfect solution delivered to your doorstep in record time. *THAT* is a perfect Message to Market Match.

What makes it even more powerful is that they entered the conversation going on inside their prospect's head, which in simple terms could be boiled down to "Hungry. Food. Now."

Had they instead focused on "delicious sauce, Mama's old country recipe, ingredients sourced from the finest all-organic farms, delivered in style by a man in a tuxedo..." it would have tanked. Because that's *NOT* what the market was looking for, and it certainly didn't match the dialogue taking place in that college kid's mind as he was watching the TV or studying for finals.

Another key mistake many make involves the language used in the marketing. When you focus on a specific group of people, you're able to tap into the vocabulary they use every day. Doing so is critical;

for example, with musicians (and magicians) you would want to promise them "more gigs," not "more jobs." Golfers have a vernacular all their own as well, with "bunkers," "buried lies," "shanks," and "skulled shots, a.k.a. wormburners." Just like you wouldn't attempt to communicate with a French person in Mandarin Chinese, you don't want to use "outsider" language and terminology when communicating a sales message to your prospective patient.

To our 1970s pizza-eating college student now approaching seasoned-citizen status, it's not about hearing a little better; that's not worth spending the money on. He can crank up the sound system, and the Rolling Stones will sound as good as ever. The real problem, which *IS* worth investing in, is not hearing what my kids are saying, them thinking I'm losing my mind because I'm not responding, and them then sending me off to the old folks' home because of that.

> You need to know more than just their demographics; you need to know their hopes, dreams, fears, and most importantly, the conversations that are going on in their heads—the things they will never tell you.

You only know this when you truly know your *WHO*. You need to know more than just their demographics; you need to know their hopes, dreams, fears, and most importantly, the conversations that are going on in their heads—the things they will never tell you.

MISTAKE #3: ASKING THEM TO
DO THE WRONG THINGS

This boils down to asking for the sale too quickly without first narrowing down our universe of potential buyers.

We live in an extremely skeptical age. Once-respected professions and institutions now have practically zero credibility, including journalists, clergy, education providers, and so many more. And even lower than politicians rank the oily, slimy salesman who's all too eager to shake your hand and pluck your purse.

Agreeing to something as potentially involved as implants, cosmetic dentistry, or even just coming in for a cleaning—particularly given all the other factors associated with choosing any one specific dentist—requires asking a person to take a leap of faith. Without first establishing a significant level of trust in your credibility, responsibility, and authority right from the get-go, you face a significant uphill battle enticing anyone to do anything, let alone sign on the dotted line.

Therefore, instead of going right for the sale out of the gate to everyone on the planet, a more effective marketing strategy is to first narrow down your focus by getting a subset of your potential market to qualify themselves by "raising their hand" in response to an offer that's much easier to say yes to—a free gift of some sort, possibly a video or a report. This enables you to begin that process of gathering a group of people who have a very specific problem or condition that you can treat. It enables you to begin establishing credibility, authority, and trust, turning an unknown potential patient into a self-acknowledged "lead" with whom you can follow up more intensely and personally.

We call this concept *"lead generation,"* and we'll discuss it in much greater detail in just a bit.

MISTAKE #4: THINKING YOU CAN ADVERTISE ANYWHERE AND EVERYWHERE

Marketing used to be relatively simple when it came to choosing which media platform to use. CBS. NBC. ABC. PBS. Local radio. Local newspapers. Yellow Pages. A limited number of high-profile magazines. Billboards. And the few other outlying options of varying effectiveness, such as skywriting, smoke signals, and a strange new technology that was called the World Wide Web.

As the giant reptiles vanished from our planet, so too has disappeared this once-simple media menu. Today, you as a marketer face a far more complicated, diverse, and challenging array of options from which to choose. New media channels and technologies seem to appear daily.

This constantly changing media landscape challenges even the most tech-savvy marketer. Not only do you have to keep up with the latest and greatest, but you also face disruptions caused by shifting public opinion, government intervention, and even changes to corporate strategy. Google adjusts its search algorithms continuously, potentially rendering an easily found, SEO-optimized website practically invisible. In regard to Pay-Per Click (PPC) ads, whole businesses were destroyed when the infamous "Google Slap" completely shut down lead-generation ads and systems that previously delivered handsome returns.

Because of this overwhelming complexity, many dentists simply throw up their hands and hand this task over to a so-called expert or ad salesman and then write the checks based on them saying, "You have to be on *x*."

The only way to avoid this mistake is to nail down exactly the *WHO* you are selling to. Once you know that, it's actually quite simple to choose which media channels to advertise in: you go where they go.

If they're on Facebook, you go on Facebook. If they read *Model Railroader*, you advertise in *Model Railroader* (and note: what you sell inside *Model Railroader* doesn't even have to relate in the slightest to trains; it just needs to appeal to the kind of person who reads that magazine).

And even though many consider them outdated, the Yellow Pages can still offer huge benefits if they're targeting an older demographic who relies on their use.

You want to only be where your *who* is, and then you want to be EVERYWHERE they are.

It's a huge mistake to try to sort out all the different options for media without first having a plan for what you intend to use that media for. The worst thing you can do is undertake a series of random, disconnected marketing attempts across various media channels. Instead, you want to create a true system that attracts new patients in an organized way. Because it's only with this kind of system that you can achieve reliable, predictable results, so you know when you invest X, you will get Y in return.

> The worst thing you can do is undertake a series of random, disconnected marketing attempts across various media channels.

MISTAKE #5: NO MARKETING SYSTEM

This is probably one of the biggest, most widespread mistakes made: marketing without a system.

Without a system you are flying blind, throwing Jell-O against a wall, seeing if any of it sticks. And if, by happenstance, something does work, you have no way of leveraging that data because anything that did produce a positive result is now an oozing green puddle on the office floor.

Without a system, you're forced to pray for and then rely on one-hit wonders (remember the "Macarena"?), which offer you a brief moment in the sunshine of success, but then vanish like dust in the wind. It worked, but you don't know why, you can't repeat the process, and once it's gone, it's gone.

This goes hand in hand with what I call "Rollercoaster Marketing" – where when times get tough and patients are scarce, you throw everything plus the kitchen sink into your marketing efforts. If you're lucky, and manage to catch a bit of traction, your funnel gets filled up, and your practice starts the ascent. So you drop everything and get to work, because you're now too busy to market, and the inevitable perception is that you don't need to because everything's fat and happy. But this only delays the inevitable, because when you stop marketing, your funnel will eventually dry up—new leads stop coming in, existing patients move on—so you start the descent, howling all the way to the bottom. And you're back to where you started.

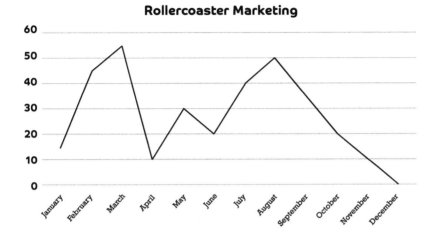

Having a reliable, scientific, predictable marketing system is what you must put in place instead. You want a system where marketing works like a faucet that you can turn on or off, depending on the needs of your practice and where you want to go with it.

At a minimum, you want your Marketing System to focus on three key areas:

1. Lead generation: The ongoing acquisition of leads for your practice

2. Conversion: Taking those leads and converting them into paying patients

3. Retention/referral: Keeping that patient base intact and generating new leads based on referrals

Once you have this system set up, you simply put it in motion and let it run. I have clients who have Magnetic Marketing Systems that have been running untouched for seven to ten years.

MISTAKE #6: CHASING PATIENTS

Almost as big a mistake as not having a system is the wrongheaded perception by dentists of all stripes that it's your job to CHASE patients. While it may seem logical to do so, ponder the implications on a personal level for a moment…

> → **Q:** What's your natural impulse when you see someone following you in hot pursuit?
>
> → **A:** You skedaddle.

And that's what your prospective patients will do once they see you chasing after them. And no matter what kind of shape you're in, they can outrun and outlast you. You will wind up left in their dust… undoubtedly along with the rest of your fellow competitors, because it's almost certain they don't know any better either.

I recommend a different approach. Stop chasing. Start attracting. Lay out something they would value as "bait" to magnetically attract them, and that will cause them to take notice and request information from you. This bait could be as simple as a two-page report promising to solve a specific problem they face or a free consumer guide. (You do this based on your research and how well you understand them, your who.)

This idea of having them come to you flips everything around and changes the game. Using this kind of approach, where you offer something of value for free in exchange for getting someone to step forward, raise his/her hand, and say, "I'm interested in learning more," gives you the opportunity to separate yourself from the competition and it completely reverses the power position of who's chasing whom.

When you stop chasing, you no longer have to resort to gimmicks (like slashing your prices or Grouponing specials) to set yourself apart from the pack of hungry competitors running alongside you. They are magnetically attracted to you.

When you use attraction, this allows you to charge and collect premium fees. People pay more for a solution that they've already at least partially embraced, or better yet—asked for.

> **People pay more for a solution that they've already at least partially embraced, or better yet—asked for.**

Attraction brings to you patients who are more committed and likely to remain with you over the long term. Another benefit is that patients who come to you through attraction are naturally inclined to remain with you and do business with you over and again.

Attraction also builds trust, which is key to making sales in our exceedingly skeptical age. The patient attraction system we recommend with Magnetic Marketing establishes your credibility and authority by delivering the results—initially on a small scale—exactly as promised, laying the foundation for even bigger sales and greater trust as you continue to deliver real value.

Attraction enables you to sell exactly what they want to buy because it ONLY draws in prospects who fit your criteria and mindset. You know them inside out, you know what they want, you attract them with something that you know works, and they'll buy and keep buying.

So what kind of marketer do you want to be? Constantly chasing after people who may or may not want you? Or calmly waiting and watching as eager new prospects knock on your door and ask for the help only you can provide?

MISTAKE #7: THINKING YOU HAVE THE AD BUDGET OF COCA-COLA

It's only natural to think the advertising you should emulate is what you see every day on TV. Because that's where the big ad dollars get spent and by the biggest, most respected brands in business like GE, GM, Google, Apple, Microsoft, Kellogg's, Anheuser-Busch, and Coca-Cola.

Millions pour into the coffers of ad agencies to produce high-definition, high-dollar commercials for the itching eyeballs of the nation. With these ads, they hope to move us emotionally, to make us laugh, and to make us associate their brands with happy feelings so that when the time comes to make a relevant buying decision, we choose them.

That's the game they're playing. And the cost to join them at the table is enormous. Most small businesses have nothing even remotely close to the ad budgets of these companies. In 2017, Coca-Cola's advertising expenses were $3.96 billion.

Do you really want to play that game too? You're not Coca-Cola. You're not going after every parched throat on the planet. You don't need to copy what they do with your advertising.

You need to do what works for you.

MISTAKE #8: RACE TO THE BOTTOM IN LOW PRICE

When you don't have a real system in place to market your practice or services, you tend to look at what your competitors are doing to build up their practices, and nine times out of ten, it's lower prices.

This occurs in practically every industry, every marketplace, from ice cream to IT: a mad dash to the bottom in the hopes that lower prices will give you the edge you need.

The only problem with this is the simple fact that there can only be ONE lowest-priced offering. Someone's got to take the hit to be number one in that race. But pole position is easy to come by, especially if you have deep pockets and you don't care if you lose money over the short term. You can afford to drive the competitors out of business.

Then congratulations, you're King.

Until you're not.

Bottom dwelling is *NOT* the path to long-term success.

MISTAKE #9: THERE'S NO FOLLOW-UP

I see this all the time, and—even though I know better than to invest any emotional energy into the exercise—it still drives me crazy.

The wife and I decide to go out to eat. We always eat at a few tried-and-true establishments, but what the heck, let's try someplace different.

So we head into town and see a new restaurant has just opened up. It looks OK from the outside. The parking lot isn't full, but it isn't empty either, so we decide to give it a try.

We go in, get seated, the waiter arrives and asks for drinks and then our order. Food arrives; it's actually better than expected. There's a nice dessert menu, followed by some coffee (equally good), and then the check and a tip, and we're out the door.

Overall, a relatively pleasant, enjoyable experience from start to finish.

That was our perception.

But we'll probably *never* return.

Why? Because they didn't seem to notice we even existed.

Sure, all the basic functions of a restaurant were executed properly—waitstaff, food service, cooking, accounting, and so forth.

But they missed the *ONE* thing that could make or break their business: they put zero effort into doing everything they could to make sure of our return.

There was no capture of name, address, even email.

There was no offer of a bounce-back coupon to entice us to come back.

They didn't ask about our anniversary, our birthdays, children, friends—none of that.

ZERO effort went into knowing us as anything but an ephemeral visitor out of the blue who showed up one night and then passed like a ship out to sea, never to be heard from or seen again.

Tragic.

THE ANSWER IS SIMPLE

When you truly know your *WHO*, you can magnetically attract all the patients you can handle. And you don't have to do this by slashing your prices, chasing after everyone in hopes of catching someone, or spending yourself into oblivion trying to imitate massive multinationals with marketing budgets greater than half the world's GDP.

You can't afford to make any of these mistakes, and you don't have to—because it's not about you; it's about them, knowing them and their needs inside and out and then meeting them exactly where they live with just what they've been looking for.

Getting the right Message…via the right Media…to the right Market…it all starts with knowing your *WHO*.

CHAPTER 3

What Happens When You Attract Instead of Chase?

When you run a dental practice, whether you're checking emails, looking at web-based appointment requests, or sitting in your office listening for the front desk phone, the worst feeling in the world is the same:

Silence.

Without a constant flow of leads and patients coming in, your practice is doomed to fail.

It doesn't matter how good you are, how motivated you are, how wonderful your clinical skills are—none of that matters. The lifeblood of every dental practice is LEADS and PATIENTS and the beauty of Magnetic Marketing is that you don't have to suffer in silence any longer.

Instead, you allow your SYSTEM to magnetically attract them to you—prequalified, prescreened, already interested in you and what you have to offer.

And don't let the word *"SYSTEM"* scare you. What you'll discover in this book is simple to understand and straightforward to implement, even if you don't have any kind of technology background.

It's all about NOT chasing patients anymore; it's about *ATTRACTING* them instead by doing the following:

→ Abandoning strategies that everyone else is using that just don't work

→ Making *MARKETING* your practice and
   your message your #1 priority

→ Focusing your marketing on the needs and
   dreams of the patients you want to attract

The difference can be dramatic, as you'll see in these stories of dentists like you who switched from marketing like everyone else and instead took that first step to implementing Magnetic Marketing principles for themselves.

Dr. Dustin Burleson opened his practice in 2006 with the mindset that "you get your degree, do good work, and like the *Field of Dreams*, the patients will come."

It didn't work out quite as he expected. He soon discovered his practice had one employee and zero patients. In fact, to pay that employee, he had to work as an associate at another practice!

Nevertheless, he persisted, and after working six days a week for about three years, he managed to grow his practice largely through blood, sweat, and tears. It worked, but it was definitely no way to live or raise a family.

Looking for ways to escape the hamster wheel and build a better practice, Dr. Burleson stumbled upon a book that opened his eyes to the power of Magnetic Marketing, realizing "this is so stupid, simple, and clear. Why haven't I been doing this?"

He finally understood that he wasn't in the business of being a doctor; he was actually in the business of *MARKETING* his practice.

This was a revolutionary concept because when it comes to dentists and their staff, most of them have never been exposed to accurate thinking on running a practice and marketing. It applies all throughout the professional services, where you're taught in dental school or medical school or law school, a lot of times, that marketing is bad and it's not something you should do; it's beneath you as a professional.

Instead, you're told that you should be as good as you can possibly be.

But the cold, hard truth is that it doesn't matter how good you are. You could be the best lawyer, the best dentist, or the best orthodontist in the world. But if you can't get the message out to the public, no one will ever get a chance to experience how wonderful you are.

So when *Dr. Burleson got into the mindset of being in the marketing business*—focusing on attracting the perfect patients to his practice—he finally managed to break through to a point where success wasn't solely dependent on working ninety hours a week.

His practice has gone from four chairs in one small clinic to four locations with five doctors, and from one employee to thirty-five employees.

Most telling of all—from zero patients to over 7,500 active patients.

In 2006, **Dr. Brian Bergh** was having an entrepreneurial midlife crisis.

No longer feeling joy in his practice, Dr. Bergh was self-evaluating whether to continue or find a new profession. "The practice became a burden that I had to go in every day and continue to do the exact same thing over and over again," Dr. Bergh revealed. "To the point where I was seriously considering not continuing in the profession."

Prior to starting his practice in 1992, he had worked in his father's practice since the age of thirteen. "When you spend that much time investing in something, it's hard to justify moving into a new area," Dr. Bergh said. But things needed to change, as it was affecting his personal life too. "I remember my wife was kind of questioning what was going on in my life because I don't think I was very happy at home either."

A big Zig Ziglar fan, Dr. Bergh saw that Zig would be a featured speaker at the Magnetic Marketing SuperConference. "I went primarily to see Zig and then fell in love with the Magnetic Marketing style of marketing and ideas they were proposing," Dr. Bergh recalled.

"The Magnetic Marketing presentation actually sparked something in me. There was no question that I agreed. It made sense to me. It was different, something that people were not doing. And it gave me a new creative outlet to restore my interest in the profession that I had chosen…to take something that had become commonplace…and to learn."

A consummate learner who reads constantly, Dr. Bergh recalled buying all the *No B.S.* books Dan Kennedy had written and being excited to read the newsletters. "I became very interested in the idea of persuasion," Dr. Bergh said. "In oral health, we're in the business of persuasion, which I didn't realize at the time. I'm using different types of persuasion techniques to move people forward for what's best for them. I found Dan's teachings in regard to sales, along with the marketing aspect, helpful and something that I enjoyed. I have many of the training programs that Magnetic Marketing has to offer."

At the time Dr. Bergh joined the Magnetic Marketing community, he had five employees and started 120 new patients a year. Today, he has twelve employees and starts 500 patients a year; plus his revenue quadrupled.

Dr. Bergh's passion for his practice was reignited. "Magnetic

Marketing saved me," Dr. Bergh said. "I don't know what I would have done if I hadn't gotten that inspiration and created a fun environment for myself. I've enjoyed marketing ever since I got involved with Magnetic Marketing. It stimulates a different part of my mind, and it's kept me sane and excited about what we do."

An added bonus came about when Dr. Bergh brought his son, Bryley, with him to multiple Magnetic Marketing events, including Young Entrepreneurs. "He was nine and came and sat in the front row with me," Brian recalled. "Now he's in the business school at USC [University of Southern California] and credits going to those conferences with stimulating his interest in business. It was something that he and I could do together and allowed us to bond as a father and son."

THE PROOF IS IN THE PUDDING

I'll acknowledge that there are so many people running around touting the next big thing that it's become harder to know whom to listen to and whom to trust.

As they say, the proof lies in the pudding.

These stories represent just the tip of the iceberg, representing the thousands of lives changed for dentists and other entrepreneurs of all shapes and sizes since the first version of Magnetic Marketing was released over twenty-five years ago.

The difference was dramatic—all because they made the shift from "Chasing Patients" to "Attracting Patients."

Even though some of the specific examples used have changed due to new forms of media emerging, the foundational principles remain solidly in place and continue to run like clockwork: attracting slam-dunk patients to your practice.

And the good news is that with the ever-expanding number of media options now available, it's never been easier to put together a Magnetic Marketing System customized perfectly for *YOU*.

Note: Now you might be saying to yourself, "But wait, my practice is different...what if I am in the commodity business? I *HAVE* to price my services lower than anyone else in order to get the business I need."

First off, your practice is *NOT* different. Dentistry is *NOT* different. Every industry faces the pressure to lower prices; one of the easiest ways to differentiate yourself in the marketplace is to announce yourself as the lowest-priced option.

If this is the route you choose to follow, I wish you the best. But understand, it's only a matter of time before someone else emerges to go after your patients with an even lower-priced option. Then you'll be forced to either lose those patients or instead, compete in a downward spiral to oblivion. It's a race very few can win and almost never for long.

The beauty of Magnetic Marketing lies in the way it sets YOU apart from the competition in a way that's focused on features/benefits you control—and that make you a UNIQUE solution to the challenges your perfect patient faces. In essence, you eliminate price as the key component in the buying decision, and in reality, most buyers place price lower than other factors to be considered, such as convenience, quality, guarantee, and so on.

Magnetic Marketing frees you from the danger of relying on pricing alone to make the sale. Even in industries where there's significant price pressure, it's almost dead certain that patients exist to pay you what you're worth.

All you have to do is identify and magnetically attract them.

CHAPTER 4

What This Actually Looks Like

Marketing is often viewed as a mysterious but necessary evil, as in, "It's definitely not the practice; it's something I have to soil myself with in order to make my practice work."

You are here because you are willing to reconsider that entire paradigm. It makes you a rare bird, soon to take flight way above all others.

The need for more leads and more patients for lifeblood exists in practices of all shapes and sizes, but few dentists ever develop formal, organized marketing systems to meet this need.

Instead, they constantly seek out the one magic bullet that will solve this problem...SEO, pay-per-click, social media, TV, billboards, radio, print ads. They hope that someone will provide the answer.

The biggest mistake made is they immediately focus on the media without having a plan or a system in mind first. They are often sold media and pour money into redoing all their websites or making new videos for them, into buying online traffic, into some "one thing" to change everything.

I call these random and erratic acts and disconnected investments "attempted marketing."

You need to realize that most ad agencies and most media representatives have a great understanding and reliance upon what's called *"Image"* or *"Institutional" advertising.*

It's what I call Goodyear blimp advertising.

When Goodyear flies a blimp over a stadium, they don't have

any illusion that at halftime of the football game, thirty-five thousand people are going to jump up out of their seats and run out and buy snow tires. They don't expect that to happen, and it's a good thing they don't, because obviously it doesn't.

What they're hoping for and what they're buying is that, over a long period of time, by these sports fans seeing the Goodyear blimp over and again, they connect it with this happy, pleasant event, and they have warm, nice, fuzzy feelings for Goodyear. Then, someday, when they have to go buy a tire, all of that comes together in their mind and causes them to buy a Goodyear tire.

I call that high-risk marketing. It just seems to me that there's a straighter line to get from a person who needs tires to buying Goodyear tires than going through all of that rigmarole of building a blimp and hiring a pilot and finding a football game and flying the blimp over it.

There is—and it's called *"Direct Marketing"* or *"Response-Driven Marketing"* or—when integrated into a complete system of attracting and converting leads—*Magnetic Marketing.*

This approach is derived from what used to be called mail order.

The discipline of the entire mail order industry—now the direct marketing industry—is that for every dollar invested there is a direct, typically fast, and always measurable return of that dollar plus presumably some profit. You can boil it down to two very basic ideas:

1. Spend $1 on marketing; get back $2 or $20 fast that can be accurately tracked back to the initial $1 invested.

2. Do *NOT* spend $1 on any marketing or advertising that does not directly and quickly bring back $2 or $20.

Go back and reread these two steps. Make sure you fully grasp this life-changing principle. They should affect *EVERY* action you take from this point forward when it comes to marketing your practice.

It's not new, and it's almost certain that you've seen, heard, or read examples of it on television, radio, letters, and so forth for most, if not all, of your life. Maybe you have even participated in it without knowing it.

Most media and ad agency people have little or no understanding of that kind of advertising and marketing. Most even fear it because it is so accountable.

To make this system work, however, the first thing you must understand in depth is *WHO* your patient is. Because even the best possible offer made to someone who is wholly unqualified, or wholly disinterested in it, is not going to work. It will fall on deaf ears.

Therefore, you've got to match your offers with precisely the right people.

KNOWING THE *WHO* IS THE MOST IMPORTANT THING YOU'LL DO

There's a story about legendary copywriter Gary Halbert, who once asked a room of aspiring writers, "Imagine you're opening a hamburger stand on the beach—what do you need most to succeed?" Answers included "secret sauce" and "great location" and "quality meat." Halbert replied, "You missed the most important thing: *a STARVING CROWD.*"

Your job is to find that "starving crowd" who can't live without what it is you have to offer.

What we want to do in terms of targeting is to find good prospective patients for our practice who can be reached affordably, who are likely to buy, who are able to buy, and preferably who already know of us or are likely to trust us.

> **Your job is to find that "starving crowd" who can't live without what it is you have to offer.**

Once you get this down and you nail exactly who your slam-dunk patient truly is— the person you absolutely want to do business with over and over again—then you'll be able to make your marketing "magnetic" because you'll be using words and phrases that'll attract your target audience. This makes your job much easier, because you can talk to them using language they relate to about what it is they really want.

WHAT YOUR WHO REALLY WANTS

Knowing exactly what your perfect patient wants is *NOT* as simple as it might seem. For example, there's the old story of the guy walking into the hardware store looking for a 3/4" drill bit. The mistake that's easily made is thinking the customer wants a 3/4" drill bit.

Wrong. *He wants a 3/4" hole.* The drill bit is just the hoop he has to jump through to get it.

Let's take it a step further than recognizing the "want" for a 3/4" hole…what's the underlying need driving *THAT* desire? Is it simply to hang a picture? Or does our homeowner crave a lifestyle surrounded by elegance that makes their home the envy of family, friends, and coworkers? So it's not just about merely needing a hole; it's about Pride and an increased sense of Self-Worth.

That's a much deeper longing, and tapping into *THAT* is where you want to connect with your *WHO*. You want to solve their problem, not just sell them something.

It's very easy to get this wrong in your messaging.

For example, you'll see financial planners competing with one another offering estate plans. Not that there's anything wrong with estate planning; it's a definite need in the minds of many fifty-plus-year-olds. But compare the phrasing "Looking for an estate plan?" to "Interested in a solution to take care of your family when you're gone?"

That's a much stronger, more emotional way of connecting to the prospective customer using terms and phrasing that resonate with what's going on inside their heads.

Another example might concern a simple service like a children's magician, whose primary market is selling birthday party magic shows to moms. A headline that reads "Joe Blow the Magician" followed by text all about Joe is appealing if "Joe" is world-renowned (not likely). A better messaging would be "Imagine: A Birthday Party Your Child Will Remember and Treasure Forever—Guaranteed!"

That's what Mom really wants. Sorry, Joe.

When it comes to dentistry, there are two big things people REALLY want from their dentist. They will usually tell you about the first thing but not the second.

First, they don't want to feel a thing. Even those people who don't have a dramatic fear of the dentist share this desire. Dentists are associated with pain for good reason, and mouth pain is the worst. This fear of pain is deep and real for just about everyone on planet Earth, so it needs your attention.

> **What people are willing to put their fears aside for is the possibility that you can give them a smile they can be proud of.**

But what they really come to you for is *confidence.* This is the thing that they usually won't say out loud. Men and women alike just want to feel attractive. They want to feel confident when they speak and smile. So while you must address the pain issue, what people are willing to put their fears aside for is the possibility that you can give them a smile they can be proud of. Sell that deep-down confidence.

As you can tell, there's a lot to truly understanding your *WHO* and what matters most to them. It requires a lot of careful thought and analysis, but the rewards are well worth it.

Having a solid understanding is only the first step though. Now you need to connect what THEY want with what YOU have to offer. And it all takes shape with a simple triangle...

PRINCIPLES
OF MAGNETIC
MARKETING

CHAPTER 5

The Magnetic Marketing® Triangle

Now let's get to building your Magnetic Marketing System. It has three big building blocks, each of which you can imagine as one side of a triangle:

→ **Message:** A truly compelling, preferably irresistible, marketing message

→ **Market:** High-probability target marketing that identifies only those most likely to respond

→ **Media:** The most appropriate, effective combination of media used to deliver your message to your market

These three can't be placed in any kind of sequential order, because no single one is more important than the other, and none of them can function without the others. It is a closed triangle. Each feeds the others, and when they work together, it gives you enormous marketing power.

BUT you can render the triangle powerless if you get any one or more of them wrong.

For example, you can deliver the right message to the right market, but if you use the wrong media—they will never get the message nor have a chance to act on it.

Or, if you get the media and market right, but fall down when it comes to a message—the right people will get what you have to say; it's just not going to connect in the way it should.

Finally, the right message via the right media goes out to the world loud and clear—but there's nobody out there to listen.

You must get ALL three right.

This is why it's so important that you really understand each and how they must work.

MARKET

In the previous chapter, I talked about the need to find your "starving crowd" of slam-dunk patients. The idea of *NOT* going after every human who still has a pulse is probably a somewhat newer concept for many doctors. In fact, most are probably guilty of "throw mud against the wall" marketing, where you are just putting a marketing message out there and hoping that somehow the right people are going to see it or hear it.

With Magnetic Marketing, we use a very different approach. Our approach is designed to do one very important thing, and that is eliminate waste to the greatest degree possible. And to eliminate waste, we must narrow our marketing focus to only the people most likely to take advantage of the services we have to offer.

The basic way that most people choose their target market is

GEOGRAPHIC. If you have a local practice, you may say your patients come from a ten-mile radius around that practice. Some dentists don't get any more sophisticated in targeting than that.

Targeting with only geographic information is like getting on a plane and dropping flyers and hoping one hits the right person. That may be an exaggeration, but the truth is that with just some simple tweaks, you can make your geographic target marketing much more effective.

DEMOGRAPHIC information is about how old people are, how much money they have, whether they are married or single, liberal or conservative, what religion they follow, and so forth.

That's another way to define further who your ideal patient is—and you need to do this—but again it's very surface level. Geographic and demographic information is important, but we want to go even deeper than that.

PSYCHOGRAPHICS delve even deeper because they explain *why* people buy. They include information like habits, hobbies, spending behaviors, and values.

Demographics and psychographics will allow you to create your ideal patient profile—a detailed picture of people you would like to work with now and in the future. So how do you determine psychographics of your target market? Here are some questions to ask yourself:

→ What keeps them awake at night, staring at the ceiling, unable to fall asleep as it relates to your services?

→ What are they frustrated about?

→ What is causing them pain right now,
as it relates to your services?

→ What is the single biggest problem
that you can solve for them?

→ What do they secretly, privately desire most?

The last question is very important. For example, most people who sell marketing courses always talk about making more money and getting more patients; they think THAT is the core desire for many dentists. But there's a deeper reason—for them and for everyone.

How do you determine your market's secret and private desires? If you've been in your practice for a while and you think about it, you are going to come up with what it is because you know them. It helps if you think about a current or past patient you would love to clone, if possible.

If not, if you are just getting into a target market, one of the easiest things that you can do is go to online discussion groups and forums. Start reading what people are posting. You will be able to figure out what pain they have just by going. You will be able to see what they secretly, privately desire most.

Immerse yourself in their world. Get their trade magazines and read them. Go to their trade shows. Talk with them. Ask questions. Watch, listen, read what they say to their peers, how they talk about their lives, and what brings meaning and what causes pain. Do what you can to get inside their heads until their deepest needs and dreams become evident to you.

This is more than knowing how they feel about dentistry—this is about discovering how they feel about themselves and what they want for themselves, their families, their friends, their careers.

If you've been in their business, walked in their shoes, laughed and cried with them, then you'll begin to understand what they secretly, privately desire most.

And once you've done all this, you'll know your *WHO*.

MESSAGE

The next building block then is right message, as in:

> This is more than knowing how they feel about dentistry—this is about discovering how they feel about themselves and what they want for themselves, their families, their friends, their careers.

What do you say to your marketplace, to your past, present, and future patients that is compelling, that is magnetic, that cannot be ignored, that must be responded to, that draws them to you like a bright porch light on a dark night draws moths?

Do you have a great marketing message? Most businesses don't. A person opens a dental practice, and the message is, "We're open for business and looking for new patients."

A marketing message is a way of concisely and clearly saying to the right market, "Here's what I'm all about, and here's why you should choose me."

So you need to ask yourself, "What am I going to say to the marketplace, and why is what I say going to be interesting and appealing to the marketplace?"

Back in chapter 1, we talked about the need to identify and create your practice's Unique Selling Proposition or USP. The example I gave was of Domino's Pizza, who built their empire based on this USP: "Fresh, hot pizza delivered in thirty minutes or less, guaranteed."

You can go out to the market with a USP like this, and you'll almost certainly do far better than most of your competitors, who are probably relying on clichés stating "the best" or "number one" or something equally meaningless.

But I'm going to take you a step deeper regarding promotional messaging—into the creation of special, highly appealing offers that I call "Widgets."

What's a Widget?

We call these very special offers 'Widgets,' and the best way to think of it is an offer on steroids.

For example, consider the owner of a hotel. A common offer might be: "Get 10 percent off your hotel room rate."

A **widget**, however, ups the ante by tossing in extra elements to make it even more attractive, hard to resist, and impossible to compare against competitors. You can think of widgets as packages of services and goods, premiums, and experiences bundled together, given a clever name, and promoted as a special, one-of-a-kind buying opportunity. So now, instead of creating an offer like "Get 10 percent off your hotel room rate" (this is frankly pretty boring and easy to ignore), compare it to something like this, which you might see instead:

Your Ultimate Weekend of Food and Fun for Only $XXX!

- □ **Ten percent savings on regular two-night room rate.**
- □ **Free gourmet dinner for two both nights.**
- □ **Complimentary bottle of champagne when you arrive.**
- □ **Limo service from and to the airport—no charge.**
- □ **Eighteen holes of golf for two, plus cart.**
- □ **Movie tickets for two, plus popcorn to boot.**
- □ **Limited availability; reserve your spot before midnight tomorrow!**

Now that's hard to ignore, especially when presented to the right person at the right time, with the right media.

Widget-making is an important marketing skill. Once you've got it, you'll use it regularly and every day in your practice. That's why it's so critical to understand the concept.

On a simple level, if we consider a pediatric dental practice, they could create a widget themed to coincide with the end of summer and back to school, and school photos. It could include a full oral exam, teeth cleaning, and a bonus package including toothbrush, toothpaste, floss, and a quality picture frame to hold that year's school photo—all for a special, one-time-only low price with highly flexible scheduling available.

They're not just saying, "Come visit the dentist."

They're saying, "Come in now to get the *Kick Off the School Year with the Brightest Smile Ever* package."

That special deal is their widget, which, until the school year actually starts, they can promote via email, flyers, TV ads, newspapers, phone scripts, on and on.

One of the best examples of widget creation that I've seen and that I know quite a bit about, comes from Las Vegas in the hotel and casino business, where pretty much everybody offers the same thing: a place to come and lose a lot of money and have a good time doing it with a lot of lights and pretty girls. For decades, that was the business in Las Vegas.

Years ago, an amazing entrepreneur, Bob Stupak, took over the worst and last hotel on the Strip. He had to find a very different way to get people to come and stay at that hotel and gamble in that casino.

He didn't have a tremendous amount of money at the time to do advertising and marketing, so the conventional ways that Las Vegas hotels market themselves were pretty much out for him.

Bob sat down and turned the hotel business and the casino business in Las Vegas into a very specific widget that he could hold up and people could see and get a grip on and understand and be attracted to and buy in advance of use.

Let me describe his widget. Ask yourself if you would respond to it, presuming you were convinced it was real.

> "Give me $396, and I'll give you two nights and three days in my hotel in one of the deluxe suites. There will be a bottle of champagne waiting for you when you arrive. You can have unlimited drinks the entire time you're here, whether you're gambling or not. Even if you're sitting in one of the lounges and enjoying the entertainment, you pay nothing more for your drinks. More importantly, for your $396, I'm going to give you 600 of my dollars to gamble with in my casino."

His widget included the room, it included the drinks, it included some extras like the champagne and souvenir dice and show tickets. It included $600 to gamble with while you were at his casino.

This widget turned that little hotel, which at the time that this started was on a Motel 6 level, into one of the largest and fastest-growing hotels on the Las Vegas Strip in its time called *Bob Stupak's Vegas World*. It eventually became *The Stratosphere*.

If you're old enough, you may recall seeing Bob's full-page ads for this widget in *Parade*, in *Sports Illustrated*, in *Playboy*, in dozens and dozens of magazines and newspapers all across the country.

Bob filled his rooms by selling that widget, and that was really the business that he was in: the business of selling that widget. He didn't advertise any other type of accommodations. He didn't bother advertising his hotel as a hotel. He concentrated all his efforts and all his energy and all his resources on *selling that widget*.

These packages were prepaid. You bought your $396 package today, but you might not actually make reservations and go to the hotel until a month later, six months later, even a year later. In the interim, Bob exchanged your $396 for a certificate, a piece of paper which entitled you to all the benefits that I described. He had your $396 in a bank account earning interest or funding construction and remodeling during that time that it was not redeemed.

If you study that example closely, you see that a fairly mundane and ordinary business, the hotel business and the hotel casino business, was turned into a totally different business.

A different business was invented within the business, and that new and different business became the widget that was sold to the public.

That's exactly the thinking process that you need to go through.

Creating Irresistible Offers

Bob Stupak's "widget" created an empire for him because, at the time, it was irresistible.

With this widget, he managed to create a *Godfather*-level kind of offer—the kind of offer you simply cannot refuse.

Think about it: this offer, this deal, it just sounded too good to be true—room, champagne, unlimited booze, even $600 in gambling money (which had to be played at the casino; it couldn't be redeemed for cash). The total package just seemed amazing.

THAT is the kind of thinking you need to put into place when creating your offers. Too many dentists come up with an offer that's practically invisible—"Save $50!" or something else that involves zero imagination and barely moves the needle.

An irresistible offer (again, think "widget," because that's what you'll be promoting) bundles together a variety of elements—price, bonuses, guarantee, speed, security, etc.—into something unique and compelling. Frankly, if the widget you create doesn't cause you to pause and reflect to yourself "Am I giving away the farm here?" for at least a moment, then the offer isn't good enough.

To be truly irresistible, it should literally overwhelm the prospect with value.

Now that doesn't mean you have to take a bath on the deals you make. Quite the opposite. Stupak watched his numbers, and he knew exactly what kind of ROI he got from every room key handed out. He also factored into the mix things like food, house winnings, return visits, referrals, and much more.

So the widget didn't stand alone; it was just one piece of a much larger play he had going involving his business and how he could maximize the lifetime value of every customer.

When creating your offer widgets, in the Magnetic Marketing System, there are three types of offers.

→ **Lead-Generation Offers**

→ **Consultation Offers**

→ **Direct Purchase or Final Offers**

Each type of offer serves a specific purpose in building a positive relationship with your prospective patient, establishing credibility and trust, all leading to the end goal of making the sale. Let's talk about each in a bit more detail.

Lead-Generation Offers

This is an offer whose only purpose is to, in effect, entice a prospect to raise their hand to identify and register themselves as having interest in certain subject matter and information or goods or services, and to invite further communication with you. Often, although not always, the lead-generation offer is free.

You see, lead generation is done by direct marketers routinely and regularly. You may not have given them much thought before, but now that you're aware of this kind of offer, you will.

For example, a national company may offer walk-in bathtubs for the elderly, advertising on cable and in national print offering their "lead gen widget," which is a free information kit and DVD. Once someone raises their hand and requests this "kit," the company now recognizes them as "raising their hand," and they can follow up with focused marketing looking to make the sale.

This model is widespread across all kinds of industries, including pharmaceuticals, finance, home improvements, and many more.

Oddly enough, you rarely find a local company doing this same strategy. Instead, they immediately try to get the prospect to commit to a "free in-home estimate" or "free consultation."

This can quite often be a mistake, as it's asking too much too soon.

"Why?" you wonder...well, Arnold Taubman, one of America's most successful mall developers, coined the term "Threshold Resistance" in regard to the entrances to retail stores. I find it applies even more broadly to direct marketing.

Again, remember that your prospect doesn't want to pull out their credit card. They don't want to get off the couch. They don't want to even pick up their cell phone and punch in a number. At a mall, it's hard enough to get them to enter a retail store where, God forbid, they face the very real possibility of some stranger walking up and trying to sell them something.

So jumping right into "Sign up for a free diagnostic consultation!"—whether from a dentist, financial advisor, remodeler, what have you—is a *BIG* threshold to get them to cross.

That's why starting with something that has a very low barrier to entry—like "Call this number and get my free report and DVD"—is much easier to convert and provides a higher response. There's less perceived risk, so those interested are more likely to respond. And by getting them to agree to that first step, albeit a tiny one, you increase the chances that further down the road, they'll become a patient. *This is a key to magnetically attracting patients.* The addition of lead generation to your marketing system allows you to create a pool of ideal people to directly market to.

Therefore, because dentistry (particularly cosmetic, including Invisalign and implants) does in fact require some sort of consultative-based sales, it's wise to get the ball rolling with an appropriate lead-generation offer of a free report or DVD or audio.

Don't ignore this strategy if the majority of services provided by your practice do *NOT* require a consultation. Remember, you have skepticism to overcome with every patient to get them to pick up the phone to schedule that appointment, whether the tooth is hurting or not.

For example, you could offer a free report laying out "7 Easy Ways to Keep Your Smile Healthy Between Dental Visits."

We call this report or DVD or whatever a Lead-Generation Magnet, and I'll go into more detail in an upcoming chapter.

Consultation Offers

It's important to understand the lead-generation offer, as it could very well be a foreign concept to you. However, the consultation offer is probably already familiar. Indeed, it could be the basic kind of offer you're making right now in your dental practice.

The point of a consultation offer is to compel the prospect to meet—either face-to-face in person or over the phone or the internet—to discuss their specific dental healthcare or cosmetic situation as it relates to the kind of services you can provide.

Again, do not underestimate how hard it can be to get someone— who may or may not know you—to drop everything and commit to this kind of meeting. You can couch this in all kinds of friendly terms like "free" and "no obligation" and what have you, but the bottom line is they know deep down there's going to be a sales pitch in there somewhere. They are deciding whether they want to give you an hour in their day to find out *IF* you are everything you say you will be. They need to trade an hour that could be spent making dinner, meeting with a new client, watching their child's soccer game, or even just the hour that they planned to spend reading a book to meet with you.

So you need to provide compelling copy that clearly explains the benefits (to them—not you) and clearly articulates how easy and low-impact this meeting will be, talking about the transformation that will take place *AFTER* they finish the meeting with you. Here's where my earlier points about emotional copywriting come into play. You're painting a picture of how their life is lacking something now, but when they finish with you, all will be right with the world.

And at the end of your meeting, or at any other point in the marketing process—it depends on your business model and how you close the deal on your services—you present the treatment plan or other service you intend to provide.

Direct Purchase or Final Offer

Here's where you present the widget and ask for the sale.

The Direct Purchase Offer you're likely most familiar with is a straight coupon offer, either from a Valpak mailing or online from Groupon or the like. Now, I'm not a champion of simply offering discounts as a strategy, but this is definitely one option.

Another common Direct Purchase Offer, in place of or in combination with discounting, is a gift with purchase where you toss in one or more bonuses.

And as we discussed earlier, when describing how to create widgets, there are other things you could integrate to make this more appealing and to drive urgency.

It's important to note that the Direct Purchase Offer is the model used by most businesses. They go right for the sale because they don't do any of the lead generation and, even worse, fail to follow up if the initial offer doesn't get accepted.

In the Magnetic Marketing System, you can go directly for the sale—and in many cases it's the right thing to do. But we don't leave that as your only option. You can instead work your way through the sales process with multiple steps, starting with lead generation, moving on to consultation, and then finally closing the deal with your final offer.

MEDIA

So we've got a great message, we've got a great market.

Here's the next challenge.

How do you take the message you've so lovingly crafted and birthed, and deliver it via the right MEDIA to these people you've carefully selected, in a way that's effective, efficient, and affordable? How will it magnetically attract back to you the perfect prospects who are ready, able, and eager to buy and buy only from you, so you get to present your case in a competitive vacuum?

How Do You Do That?

It's incredibly challenging, even for dentists who are far more technologically astute than I. The laundry list of media options available changes practically with every breath you take. There's no possible way anyone could keep up.

So how do you choose?

Once you know your *WHO*, it's easy: *where they live is where you target.*

I know—you've been told to be EVERYWHERE for EVERYBODY.

Instead, you go everywhere *ONLY* where your *WHO* is.

→ If they're on Facebook (and Facebook has amazing capabilities to segment, divide, and conquer), then you go to Facebook.

→ If they're subscribers to a highly focused, niche magazine that's eagerly awaited every month by a dedicated fan base, then you go there.

➔ **If they're hard-core conservatives who plan their day around talk radio, then you go there.**

You do *NOT* go where they're *NOT*. It's not only unnecessary; it's also a waste of time, energy, and money. You go where they *ARE* instead.

If you make a list, you can make a long list of media, things that you can spend money on to deliver marketing messages.

These days, everyone is infatuated with the internet, and the systems that we teach work brilliantly online. But the internet is not a business. It is a medium, and it is not the only medium.

So while going online is one option, another option is to use traditional print advertising. This could mean direct mail, Valpak, Free-Standing Inserts, Yellow Pages, or Display Ads in newspapers or local periodicals.

You can go network at events. You can go on radio and television. You can put team members on the phone. On and on and on and on.

The reality is you should use a combination of all of the different media—in fact, a combination of online and offline.

Here's a couple of things you need to know.

First of all, all that stuff works, and it all can be made to work better with good direct-response methods.

But only a handful of all those things that you can do, can be converted into a system. And *SYSTEM* is one of my favorite words. System means reliable, consistent, predictable results.

You get it working once, and then it keeps working on its own for a long, long, long, long, long time before you have to tweak it again.

We need *marketing systems*.

And over the next few chapters, I'm going to lay out for you a marketing system that is so predictable, so reliable, so consistent, that when you have this working for you, you go to bed knowing—not hoping, wishing, not even praying, but *knowing*—within a small, acceptable range of variance, how many good patients are going to come to you by noon the next day, every single day, for as long as you use the system.

It's like a thermometer. You can even turn it up or down to get more or less any time of the week, month or year that you want them. It's that scientific.

But there are some rules you must follow...

How Dr. Chai Got His Passion For Dentistry Back And Turned His Practice Around After Four Years Of Downward Spiral

"I became a slave to my practice," Dr. Jesse Chai recalled. "And I was making way less money than I did before…I felt like a failure."

That's how Dr. Chai, owner of Bradford Family Dentistry in Bradford, Ontario, felt after moving into his dream dental practice in 2014.

He invested $3.5 million to build and equip his new dental office. He hired a marketing director to fill the chairs. He hired associates to take on the extra workload and expanded his staff to fourteen. He did everything he was told to do. But instead of growing, he was netting much less than he used to.

With no one to guide him through this transition, he tried five different associates. None of them worked out. "I had to redo most of their work free of charge, as their dentistry was horrible," Dr. Chai said. "That affected our reputation." He was sued after terminating an associate for chasing off two families and "pissing off all of his staff." His marketing director was not delivering results, so he had to be let go too.

> He realized he'd made the mistake many entrepreneurs make… *he stopped using what consistently delivered successful results.*

Dr. Chai spiraled into a deep depression. In 2018, he decided to sell his practice and find something else to do.

By the end of the year, with no suitable buyer in sight and revenue under $2 million for the first time since 2012, Dr. Chai went back to the drawing board. He realized he'd made the mistake many entrepreneurs make…*he stopped using what consistently delivered successful results.* He reengaged with Magnetic Marketing, which had originally helped him grow from $1.1 million to $2.3 million between 2009 and 2012.

Comprehending that disengaging from his Magnetic Marketing community was the biggest mistake of his life, he not only rejoined the Magnetic Marketing community in 2019, but he also went all in—attending SuperConference and Growth Summit and joining the highest-level Mastermind Group.

"It paid off," Dr. Chai said. "I had my best year ever as a solo dentist." Not only did he increase revenue by $200,000, his net profits are healthy again, as he was able to control overhead expenditures. He paid down $250,000 of debt on the building. Plus, because he is taking vacations (including a trip to Greece, a Disney Alaskan cruise, and a trip to New York City this past year), he is feeling rejuvenated about practicing dentistry again. "I no longer regret buying the building," Dr. Chai said. "I'm taking more time off to rejuvenate than I was before. I'm a lot more engaged, and I've been taking a lot of action. This year is starting with a bang, and we are again on pace to have our best year ever."

In addition, *Dr. Chai now has emotional freedom* and no longer has a work-life balance problem. "I used to feel guilty working on the weekends," Dr. Chai said. Now he reads every day, and when nothing is scheduled on a planned personal day, he will work on his practice if he feels like it because it is enjoyable, fun, and exciting to him.

Here are the key strategies Dr. Chai used to turn his practice and his life around:

Find your why. "I did not start turning things around until I looked at my *WHY* and developed my personal vision," Dr. Chai said. "That's where it has to start."

Dr. Chai spent several weeks getting clarity and intentionally creating a vision for his life and practice. "I realized I was just going through the motions," Dr. Chai said. "That was the only way I could cope with the disappointment and stress...it was tough for me to figure out my *WHY* because, for the past six years, I had been living someone else's why. Once I nailed down my why, my vision became clearer. That was the foundation of resetting my mind. Because in order to fulfill my personal life, I had to fix the practice."

He created a twenty-page document that included his bucket list of things he wanted to do, relationships he wanted to maintain, and what he wanted to do with his family. He wrote down where he saw himself, his family, and his practice five, ten, fifteen, and twenty years from now.

Target WHO you want to work with. Changing *WHO* Dr. Chai was targeting rejuvenated him. He began focusing on patients who cared about and had the means to make good decisions regarding their dental health. Previously his patients complained a lot and always argued on price. This left him drained and made him "want to quit."

"I realized when I was working on wrong-fit patients, it was contributing to my misery," Dr. Chai said. "*By changing my marketing to focus on getting more of my ideal clients*, or at least those that had the potential to be 'A' clients, I was starting to have more fun."

Make the right offer.

Previously, Dr. Chai was using free offers to attract new patients. After speaking with members in the Magnetic Marketing community, Dr. Chai concluded that premium offers worked better than free. Instead of a free exam, he offers a free electric toothbrush when new patients pay for their first exam, x-rays, and cleaning. "We found that we're getting better patients because they come in knowing they have to pay something," Dr. Chai said.

Dr. Chai always has two offers. The generic electric toothbrush promotion is in every mailer to attract new patients, and a rotating special offer ties to a specific focus for the month, such as braces or a crown offer. Typically, he rewards patients for prepaying for a service rather than waiting for insurance to pay. "Braces are paid over several months," Dr. Chai explained. "We might offer a $500 discount if they pay in full up front. This saves them money and saves us from a ton of administrative nightmare payments."

Personality in copy. To make his messages interesting and create copy that speaks to his target market, he began applying ideas from the No B.S. *Personality In Copy* course. His messages are fun and infuse celebrity. Dr. Chai enjoys going to comic cons and conventions to meet celebrities. Therefore, he's collected a huge library of celebrity photos he can use in his marketing.

For example, he has a picture with Captain America. "I'll tell a story of when I met him during a Q&A," Dr. Chai explained. "There are questions about self-confidence, and I used what he said to resonate with patients that are not happy with their smile. Then I connect the stories and give a call to action based on that."

Go to work on the practice. In his rediscovery of Magnetic Marketing, Dr. Chai found there are resources for growing and scaling your business. "It's not just marketing; it's how to run a business," Dr. Chai said. "It goes deeper. You start with Magnetic Marketing. You get into it more, and there are other strategies such as how to deal with staff and putting systems in place." For example, at SuperConference, Dr. Chai discovered:

> "It's not just marketing; it's how to run a business," Dr. Chai said. "It goes deeper."

1. **How to create a workplace environment that breeds greatness.** After hearing Adam Witty, CEO of Magnetic Marketing and Advantage|ForbesBooks, talk about how a "great company starts with you" and how to create a great company culture, Dr. Chai followed Adam's step-by-step plan. "Adam Witty's Roadmap on a business card was eye opening," Dr. Chai said. Following Adam's advice to have a clear plan, communicate the plan, and work the plan, Dr. Chai redefined his USP, mission, core values, and strategy, involving his team as instructed. He communicated his "road map" with his team and got them to commit to the plan.

2. **Resources to execute his plan.** Dr. Chai found resources through vendors and other members he met at SuperConference that have helped him solve his problems faster.

"I got a ton out of SuperConference," Dr. Chai said. "I went back with a bunch of notes and action plans and I went to work *on* the practice."

At Growth Summit, he attended the bonus day when Adam Witty dug into creating a culture for your business and building a team that is on board. Dr. Chai finds the environment of being around "very smart business people and getting to feed off their knowledge" and hearing "Adam Witty's bonus day at Growth Summit" was "very inspiring." "When I got back, I read his book *Looking Forward to Monday*, cover to cover," Dr. Chai said. The workbook from the bonus day helped him create an effective recruiting system. Dr. Chai also created scorecards for his team and a five-year vision with his team.

Make yourself referable. The past year Dr. Chai focused on creating a referral package and program. To come up with the process, he used the *Ultimate No B.S. Referral Machine* along with the power of the Mastermind. "I showed pieces I was working on at Titanium," Dr. Chai said. "They gave me feedback." Because eight to twelve other businesses shared what is working for them and because he followed the Renegade Millionaire principle of knowing what your time is worth and outsourced the creation, Dr. Chai was able to speed up implementing a successful referral system.

Join a Mastermind Group. In addition to helping him build out his referral system, Dr. Chai said he got a lot from just listening to Mastermind members talk about their challenges. "I got a lot of good stuff from when other people did hot seats," Dr. Chai said. "For example, people were talking about employment issues they were having…I took a lot of notes that helped improve our process."

This also kept him motivated to take massive action. "You don't want to be the guy that did nothing between meetings," Dr. Chai said. "There are people in that room doing amazing things…it comes back to 'You're the average of the five people you hang around most.'"

Document your systems. Dr. Chai had no systems documented. "Magnetic Marketing was the catalyst for us to document every system we have," Dr. Chai said. "We are taking our systems and making training manuals for each department. We also are documenting any system that needs to be in those training manuals that are still missing."

The person in the office who is the most knowledgeable is tasked with documenting the process. Documents are shared on Google Drive so that they can be shared and edited as processes are improved. These manuals are "done-for-you" training for any new employee.

Dr. Chai's closing advice. "You have to start with *WHY.* Then build the practice to that, document all your systems, and then hire to your core values and train them on your systems," Dr. Chai said. "Be careful who you work with as a coach and who you take advice from, as that can be dangerous too. Especially if you are taking life-changing suggestions like buying a building or hiring other technicians—in my case, doctors—to replace you. Work with people like Magnetic Marketing who can help you, and if they can't do it themselves, it is very likely they know someone who can."

CHAPTER 6

The 10 Foundational Rules

I spend a good portion of my book, *The No B.S. Guide to Direct Marketing,* laying out the ironclad rules that will transform any dental practice into an infinitely more powerful direct-marketing business. These also are the foundational rules that govern Magnetic Marketing.

Note that these are *NOT* "recommendations"; consider them mandates. Gospel. Etchings in stone brought down at great peril from the mountain. Please copy them down and post them anywhere and everywhere you work so that they will remain at the front and center of all marketing efforts from this day forward.

Resolve now that every ad you run, every flyer you distribute, every postcard or letter you mail, every website you put up, everything and anything you do to market your practice *MUST* adhere to these rules.

Yes, they are simplistic and dogmatic, and you will undoubtedly encounter specific situations where you find there truly is a rational reason to violate one or more.

But for now, sticking to them rigidly is the right approach, the best approach, and the approach that you can be sure will work. You can experiment later, after you have gained practical experience in their use and have fully exorcised the demons of "brand advertising" from your mindset and your practice.

RULE #1: THERE WILL *ALWAYS* BE AN OFFER OR OFFERS

Number one, there will always be an offer or offers. On the internet especially, there's a popular idea that content is king. I would disagree. The sale is king.

All your marketing needs to have an offer telling your ideal prospects exactly what to do and why they want to do it right now. It should be irresistible and time sensitive and give them some kind of transformative value if they take action.

This is not just an implied offer like a store running ads: "We're here; come on in." This should not be a common offer like "The Sale of the Century! This Weekend Only!" Instead, ideally yours is a *Godfather* Offer, an offer so big, so bold, so perfectly targeted to the *WHO* you've identified as your slam-dunk patient that it is impossible to refuse.

Now this offer could be to generate a lead (with some sort of Lead-Generation Magnet like a free report, video, etc.) or to actually make the sale at that time. Needless to say, a great deal of thought needs to go into your offer, as we explained in the previous chapter.

Regardless of the nature of the offer itself, the point is to make certain that every communication actually asks somebody to do something. Focusing on this injects a new level of discipline into all of your communications with prospects, patients, and the marketplace at large.

This rule should open your eyes to the sad reality that the vast majority of advertising presented merely shows up and talks about the marketplace, the advertiser, the wind, sun, and the rain, social values, what have you, without any kind of reference to something specific to be had by immediately responding. In essence, the blimp passes by once again, fading into the sunset, leaving no trace behind. Nothing to track, nothing to measure, nothing to score. Money flies off with the wind.

When you take this kind of undisciplined approach to your marketing and simply spend and hope and guess, you're at the mercy of relying on opinion as to its effect. Do you like it? Did your mother-in-law think it was humorous and expel a chuckle? Do your patients say nice things about it? Try paying your bills with that kind of feedback.

RULE #2: THERE WILL BE A REASON TO RESPOND RIGHT NOW

The hidden costs and failures in all advertising and marketing are in the "almost persuaded."

They were tempted to respond. They nearly responded. They got right up to the edge of response, but they set it aside to do it later or to mull over or to check out other options.

When they get to that edge, we must reach across and drag them past it. There must be a good reason for them not to stop short or delay or ponder; there must be urgency.

Remember, hesitation and procrastination are among the most common of human behaviors. Your prospect doesn't want to move, period. Just like Homer Simpson, the last thing he wants is to put down the doughnut, get off the couch, and actually do something. Hence, you must provide a compelling reason to act, *NOW*.

There are plenty of ways to add URGENCY:

→ Tie the offer to a hard and fast deadline.

→ Restrict the offer to a limited number of patients.

→ Remove the bonus or gift from the
deal if they don't act right away.

→ Add an element of "bidding"
to the deal, à la eBay.

Those are just a few ideas; open your eyes to the world of experienced direct marketers out there, and I'm confident you'll discover many more. Regardless, make sure to give a reason to act *NOW*.

RULE #3: YOU WILL GIVE CLEAR INSTRUCTIONS

Most people do a reasonably good job at following directions. For the most part, they stop on red and go on green, stand in the lines they're told to stand in, fill out the forms they're given to fill out, and applaud when the applause sign comes on.

Most people are conditioned from infancy in every environment to do as they are told. Marketers' failures and disappointments often result from giving confusing directions, or no directions at all, and confused or uncertain consumers do nothing.

People rarely buy anything of consequence without being asked. You must walk your prospect through the steps you want them to take in order to make the sale.

This is far more important than you might imagine. Take to heart the old rule: "A confused buyer *WON'T* buy!" Anxiety rises anytime you ask someone to do something that they're unsure of what to expect or how to carry out.

Therefore, whenever you put together any kind of marketing tool, ad, flyer, sales letter, website, phone script, etc., make sure to examine it from the perspective of an unsuspecting patient/prospect encountering it for the very first time.

Consumers like, are reassured by, and respond to clarity. Be sure you provide it.

RULE #4: THERE WILL BE TRACKING, MEASUREMENT, AND ACCOUNTABILITY

If you want real profits from your marketing, you are no longer going to permit any advertising, marketing, or selling investments to be made without directing accurate tracking, measurement, and accountability.

Forget about likes, links, opens, shares, reach, visibility, views, and engagement—they can't be deposited in your bank account. All of that may be interesting, even indicative, but what matters is that for every dollar you spend, you can clearly identify how much comes back as a result.

This is for two reasons:

1.   Business management by objectives is the only kind of management that works.

2.   You need real, hard facts and data to make good, intelligent marketing decisions.

If you loop back and connect this to Rule #1, you'll find an important key in tracking: offers. Different offers can be made in different media, to different lists, and at different times. You can include and assign promotion codes to coupons, reply cards, websites, order forms, phone numbers, and so forth. With this data, you can determine which offers and variations of offers work best to which lists under what conditions.

Tough-minded management of marketing requires *knowing* things and then acting wisely upon what you know.

RULE #5: ONLY NO-COST BRAND-BUILDING

I am not opposed to brand-building.

I am opposed to *paying for* brand-building.

Most dental practice owners cannot afford to properly invest in brand-building. I do not believe it is a wise investment, nor do I believe it is even necessary. You can acquire all the brand power you need as a no-cost by-product of profitable direct-response advertising and marketing as described in this book.

My preferred strategy is simple: buy response; gratefully accept brand-building as a bonus. NEVER buy brand-building and hope for response as a bonus, unless you simply want to spend Daddy's fortune out of spite.

Paying for traditional brand-building may be fine, even essential, for giant companies with giant budgets engaged in a fierce combat over shelf space and consumer recognition. So if you're Coors or Heinz or some other company like that, feel free to play with the shareholders' money to buy name recognition. But if you're an entrepreneur playing with your own marbles, beware because copying what the big companies do to build their brands can bankrupt you.

Even though it is held in high regard by media companies and advertising agencies alike, "brand" is not the holy grail magically able to cure all your business woes. Brand-building is best left to very patient marketers with very deep pockets filled with other people's money. You are far better served by focusing on leads, patients, and profits directly driven by your marketing system.

RULE #6: THERE WILL BE FOLLOW-UP

People read your ad, get your letter, see your sign, find you online, etc.

They call or visit your website or practice.

They ask your receptionist or team members questions.

And sadly, in far too many cases, that's it.

There's not even the slightest attempt to capture the prospect's name, physical address, or email address. There's no offer to immediately send an information package, free report, or coupons.

This is criminal waste. I've been poor, and I abhor and detest and condemn waste.

When you fail to follow up, you are simply shrugging your shoulders and accepting waste as yet another cost of doing business. This is madness.

When you invest in advertising and marketing, you're not just paying for the patients you get. You are paying for each lead you generate, every call, every walk-in, every email, every reaction and response of any kind.

If an ad costs you $1,000 and you get fifty calls, every call you fail to follow up on is exactly like pulling a $20 bill from your wallet, taking a match to it, and watching it go up in flames. So unless you truly do have money to burn, you need to make sure to follow up with every lead that comes through your door.

There are hundreds of variations for follow-up campaigns and strategies, blending offline with online. Here are just a few ways you can follow up:

1. **Restate, Re-Sell, and Extend the Same Offer.** Present what they didn't do or buy again in the best way possible. You can do this in a straightforward manner with letters or emails. You can also use "retargeting" online technology to keep the offer in front of someone long after they've seen it the first time; they'll see it on other websites they visit, on their Facebook feed, and so on.

2. **Provide a Stern or Humorous "2nd Notice" Tied to an Onrushing Deadline.** Present the offer again, reemphasizing the approaching deadline.

3. **"Third and Final Notice."** Tie this communication to the deadline and the disappearance of the offer.

4. **Change the Offer.** Sometimes you can change the offer relatively easily, by offering new or extended installment payment terms, by swapping out a bonus for something different, etc.

Doing nothing with even one lead is like flushing money down the toilet. It is a serious lapse in judgment and waste of precious resources every time you fail to follow up with every lead and every patient.

RULE #7: THERE WILL BE STRONG COPY

The fact is, there is enormous, ever-growing, almost overwhelming competition for attention and interest—a daily tsunami of clutter that must be cut through or circumvented. In this environment, where literally tens of thousands of messages bombard your prospects every day, the ordinary and the normal are ignored, the cautious and calm messages unnoticed.

You can't send a shy, timid Casper Milquetoast to knock on the door of a home or walk into a business and beg in barely a whisper for a few moments of the prospect's time. So you can't do that with a postcard, letter, flyer, newsletter, email, video, etc., either.

You want to send the Incredible Hulk instead—huge, glowing, neon green, stomping, impossible to ignore. He shows up, and the guy drops whatever he's been doing and pays attention.

But the copy can't just shout. "Loud but irrelevant" isn't much better than "quiet yet relevant." Loud: You can grab attention, but you can't convert it to interest. The Incredible Hulk stomping into your office would get your attention, but he'd still have trouble bridging to interest and having you engage in a conversation with just about any new product.

Strong copy can be sensational and attention-commanding, but it does so in a way that establishes relevance and credible authority—creating proactive interest in our information, goods, and services. Here's a good example of a strong headline making a real benefit-oriented promise:

Find Out Why 7 Out of 10 Toothpastes Don't Stop Tooth Decay

Special report reveals the 4 key toothpaste ingredients that, if missing, can cost you your smile and even your teeth...

Most strong copy gets written backward, starting from the customer's interests, desires, frustrations, fears, thoughts, feelings, and experiences (remember the emphasis earlier on nailing down the *WHO?*)—and then journeys forward to reveal a solution tied to your business.

Most ineffective copy takes the reverse path: starting instead with the company, product or service and its features, benefits, comparative superiority, and price. This is the common default approach the overwhelming majority of advertisers, copywriters, and salespeople fall back to, rather than developing a more creative, customer-focused approach.

Here are two major mistakes your copy can't afford to make:

1. **Writing factually and "professionally" rather than emotionally.** Great copy communicates conversationally, one-on-one, just like you would sitting across the table from a friend you can't wait to let in on something wonderful you've just discovered. And it makes no difference whether you're selling to a *Fortune* 1000 CEO or Al Bundy in his trailer—your best approach is to write like you talk, speaking passionately from the heart with deeply emotional appeals.

2. **Being timid or bland in your claims and promises.** Many believe their patients are smarter and more sophisticated than others, at least immune to sensationalism and hyperbole, perhaps offended by it, and they discredit themselves by engaging in it. Wrong. These beliefs are in contradiction to facts and experience, for in every category of product or service, in media directed at presumably educated, sophisticated people, I can find examples of ads making grandiose and extraordinary claims that succeed mightily. Zig Ziglar was right: "Timid salesmen have skinny kids"—no matter whom they're selling to.

The fact you must embrace about strong sales copy is that you need it, and you may have to learn to write it for yourself. If this concept happens to be brand new to you, start with my Magnetic Marketing System, available at MagneticMarketing.com.

RULE #8: IT WILL LOOK LIKE MAIL ORDER ADVERTISING

This rule is a great simplifier, because it ends you paying attention to—and trying to emulate—the overwhelming majority of all the advertising you see on TV, in magazines, in newspapers, online, by your peers and competitors. You are to go blind to anything except *pure* mail order advertising. Anything else, shut the door, ignore.

I am specifically speaking of their formats, layout, and appearance of advertising, whether print ad or a web page or any other item.

Here's exactly the type of ad I'm talking about:

Classic mail order ads are typically broken up into one-half and one-quarter of the page, give or take. The top quarter is for headline and subheads; the middle half for presentation of product or proposition, sometimes aided by testimonials; the bottom quarter for the offer and clear response instructions, often with a coupon.

The most frequently used alternative is the advertorial, which mimics an article.

The other reliable format is that of a letter, from you to the reader, at whatever length is necessary to do the job. I have clients mailing four-, eight-, sixteen-, twenty-four, and in one case, sixty-four-page sales letters. One of these, a sixteen-page one that was literally tacked up online as a website, having traffic driven to it, has produced $1 million a year for nine years running.

To see real mail order advertising you need to assemble a diverse assortment of magazines in which highly successful mail order companies consistently run full-page advertisements. These include *Reader's Digest Large Print Edition,* tabloids like the *National Enquirer,* and business publications like *Investor's Business Daily* and *Entrepreneur.* Also check out special interest magazines for model railroad hobbyists, gun enthusiasts, horse lovers, etc., as you'll find fractional and full-page mail order ads.

Tear out and keep these ads as research; *discard all others.* Let these ads be your only models. If you respond to some, your mailbox will soon be full of direct mail that also follows classic formats and architecture.

You'll eventually have a collection of advertisements that, if studied and modeled for your own use, represent money in the bank.

If you're looking for a shortcut, I have compiled a few along the way, with templates in my *Magnetic Marketing System & Toolkit* (available at MagneticMarketing.com).

RULE #9: RESULTS RULE. PERIOD.

Results rule. Period.

Do not let anyone confuse, bamboozle or convince you that anything else is of any importance. Nobody's opinion counts—not even yours.

And there's no excuse for not assessing results anymore. With today's technology, it's easier than ever to link and track specific promotions to quantifiable results. You can even do what's called "split-testing" or "A–B" testing, where you match one headline against another to see which produces the best results, and then continue the process over and again. Test. Monitor. Adjust. The goal is to gradually achieve the very best results possible.

The only thing that matters is the answer to the question, "What results did I get?" When you implement this into your marketing approach and marketing messages, you change the way you communicate with your prospects and patients dramatically and forever.

> **NOTE:** A lot of what you have just read in the previous rules may seem weird, sound funny, or feel wrong to you. Too bold. Too aggressive. Too hype-y. Too unprofessional. Too far outside the box of what's deemed "correct" for your profession or peers. That's understandable. But it doesn't matter because, remember, *your opinions NEVER COUNT.* You don't get a vote; neither does your wife, your mother, your golfing buddy, neighbor, competitor, employee. Nobody gets a vote. The only vote that counts is the patient's, and the only legal, valid ballots are cash, checks, and credit cards.

RULE #10: YOU WILL BE A TOUGH-MINDED DISCIPLINARIAN AND PUT YOUR PRACTICE ON A STRICT DIRECT-MARKETING DIET

Many dentists who perennially struggle and suffer are very much aware of things that need doing but simply lack the will to do them.

Maybe it's a longtime vendor or team member, now a "friend," who you know is toxic and needs to be replaced, but you can't muster the will to fire them.

Maybe there's an ad that you keep spending money on that you know is failing to deliver results, but you lack the will to fix it or shut it down.

Maybe there's a website you know isn't producing, either, but the very thought of getting it remade is painful, so it stays as is.

From this point forward, with *ALL* advertising and marketing, you have to be thick-skinned about criticism, tough-minded about money invested, extremely disciplined in thought and action, and dedicated to carrying out your game plan, all fueled by a resolute will to win.

> **IMPORTANT**: *Anything* that doesn't conform to the 10 Rules discussed in this chapter, do not let in at all. Just say no. And bar the door.
>
> When you DO implement all these into your marketing approach and marketing messages, you change—for the better—the way you communicate with your prospects and patients dramatically and forever.

From Burnout To Exponential Growth & Living Life On Your Terms

How Dr. Carlo Biasucci tripled his practice, cut his hours in half, and grew his business to $8.2 Million in just three years

In 2012, Dr. Carlo Biasucci narrowly survived an injury. While on vacation with his wife, Ashlee, Carlo suffered severe decompression from scuba diving, an injury that kept him from working in his dental practice for three months.

"At that point, I realized how fragile my business was," Carlo said. "I was conventionally successful at $2.4 million, at least in my area compared to my peers, but I was unhappy. At that amount of billing, with a dentist and an associate, to get any more juice out of that machine, you've got to run faster on the treadmill. There's just no other way to do it, beyond leverage, and that's the thing I didn't have, I didn't know how to do, and I didn't think was possible."

Burned out, frustrated, and exhausted, Carlo came to the realization that his life was out of balance. "A lot of things took a back seat, which was my health, and I had not started a family yet, which was high on my list," Carlo said. "I was basically checking all of the boxes on the wrong side of the column. *I realized I hadn't really done anything I wanted to do in my life.*"

Carlo gave himself an ultimatum: fix his practice in the next twelve months or quit dentistry completely. Searching for answers, he discovered Dan Kennedy on YouTube and binge-watched everything he could find. "Dan's message of living life on your terms resonated and is exactly what I grabbed onto," Carlo said. He spent the next two years studying and implementing. "I went all in," Carlo said.

"I bought every product I could buy. I watched every video I could watch. I have bookshelves full of Dan Kennedy's material. Magnetic Marketing, books, products, everything."

Located in the steel town of Sioux St. Marie, Ontario, Canada, the economy was still recovering from the 2008 downturn. The steel mill went into bankruptcy protection, and one of the other major employers, the paper mill, went under. Despite this, Carlo tripled his practice in just three years, growing it to $8.2 million. His staff grew from fifteen team members to forty, he went from one associate and himself to nine dentists, from nine operatories to seventeen, and to serving 12,000 active patients. In the process, he cut his workweek in half, doubled his income, and started a second business, TheElite-Practice.com.

In March 2018, he sold his practice for three times what anyone has ever sold a practice for in his area. Today, he continues to work in the dental field. Putting all his focus on coaching dentists on how to implement a team-driven practice, Carlo has grown his Elite Practice business to multi-seven-figures in two years with a net higher than the most profitable year of his dental practice. He also has balance in his life now.

"It's a complete change in energy, in health, in family life," Carlo said. "All the boxes are checked. Where I was only in balance financially, I can now say everything is in place. I'm fortunate to have crossed paths with the Magnetic Marketing World. And fortunate I'm stubborn and implemented everything. I also didn't try to outthink it. I just did exactly what I was told."

The Most Influential Strategies That Changed Everything

"The biggest thing I realized when I began studying the Magnetic Marketing System and Toolkit was that my original business model sucked," Carlo said. "I thought I had systems, but everything revolved around me instead of having my team do it. And my process around marketing sucked because we were doing the traditional type of marketing."

Carlo credits reading Dan Kennedy's book *No B.S. Ruthless Management of People and Profits* for waking him up to the realization that he should not be doing everything himself.

The Power of Being Everywhere

After immersing himself in the Magnetic Marketing System and Toolkit, Carlo did a complete 180 in his marketing. After he substantially expanded the media he used to spread his message, his new patient flow increased from 45 to 175+ per month. He sustained this increased flow for the remaining five years he owned the practice and grew his database to 20,000 names in a town of 73,000. "I realized my errors and completely changed directions into an 'omnipresent direction,' as Dan Kennedy would say," Carlo said. "We were everywhere—in all media, community-based events—effectively patients were saying, 'I can't get away from you; you are everywhere.'"

> His new patient flow increased from 45 to 175+ per month.

Hosting free community events that incorporated Magnetic Marketing principles became huge lead generators and grew his list quickly. "We created a theme park in our parking lot once a month," Carlo explained. "We were drawing in the community, getting seventy new families. These weren't little—we had pony rides, go-cart races, all kinds of stuff. Everything was free, including the food. We got sign-ups, names, emails, mailing addresses…and we created a large database of prospects, which is something I'd never even heard of prior to Magnetic Marketing." After building his list, he used it to fill seminars on demand too. "An implant seminar would bring in a hundred thousand dollars for a couple of hours of work," Carlo said.

In addition, Carlo sent press releases using Magnetic Marketing components. Featured in every local media, he became a source for the news anytime there was a dental story. "This took us to the next level," Carlo said. "*We tripled and quadrupled our new patient flow.* The team got a cake and wrote '200' on it for the month that we had 200 new patients in the practice."

Position Yourself Above Competitors

"My marketing previously focused on trying to be better than the other guy, which was obviously foolish because patients don't know the difference," Carlo said. "They assume everyone with a dental degree is competent. What I picked up through Dan's message and the Magnetic Marketing world is that your differentiation point must be authority-based positioning. I became the conduit, if you will, of all things dental for my community. We became the provider of great information and therefore the assumed authority. All of our marketing continued from there with Magnetic Marketing principles."

Carlo has written seventeen free reports and five books, including *The Elite Practice,* with a foreword written by Dan Kennedy. He also created four webinars, turning them into DVDs to include in his shock-and-awe package mailed to prospective patients.

Stand Out From The Crowd

Carlo strives to implement Dan's concept of "show up like nobody else" in everything he does, from the moment they find out about him through the delivery of his service. "It's looking at every single one of a hundred touchpoints," Carlo said. "What does the industry expect, and how can we disrupt that? How could we do it better? How could we do something they weren't expecting? Those are the questions that we look at."

> What does the industry expect, and how can we disrupt that? How could we do it better? How could we do something they weren't expecting?

Increase Profitability, Patient Satisfaction, Loyalty, and Trust

Monthly newsletters are well received and create a stickiness factor with patients to this day. "Dan's always pushed retention," Carlo said. "I never paid attention to it. I always thought it was a silly waste of money to send a newsletter to people who were already my patients. But you must do something between sending them bills every six months to keep people in your world and grow the relationship. I used to keep my family and personal life separate. I realize how stupid that was now. I started sharing. I started writing…about my personal life, my family, and so on. That created incredible retention that I didn't have before. It lets people see you as a real person, rather than just the dentist."

Boost Patient Acceptance

Consistent communication keeps him top of mind, helps him stay competitive against his biggest rivals, and increases lifetime value. "When you already have people in the chair, you don't worry so much about the ones that got away," Carlo said explaining why he previously didn't follow up. *"Creating a system for follow-up for unaccepted treatment for prospective patients was another huge boost."*

Follow-up includes a simple letter, phone calls, emails, and letters from the doctor, all prompting patients to complete treatment. Carlo also includes a free report relevant to the treatment they need. "Even if someone were thinking about getting a second opinion, they were coming back to us because we wrote the book on it," Carlo said.

Identify What Works

An overarching theme is keeping track of the marketing so he can evaluate what is successful and worth repeating and what is wasting his valuable marketing budget. "Dan talks about tracking, strategic execution, and having a marketing plan," Carlo said. "We weekly, monthly, quarterly and annually plan everything in advance. That keeps us on track…shows us what is significant…and keeps us from forgetting to do successful pieces again."

Become More Efficient

By applying Dan's time management concepts, Carlo learned how to become more efficient and effective. "When I figured out how to leverage time, that was a game changer," Carlo said. "By applying this disciplined structure to my life, there has been immense freedom. As a result, I'm more productive in six hours of work than I used to be in a week's worth of work. And because of that, there's tons of free time. On a regular day, I can be free when my daughter comes home from school, and we go play outside."

Grow Faster

In November 2015, Carlo attended his first Magnetic Marketing event. This led to a private session with Dan Kennedy and launching his info-business within just six months. "I'd already seen the first doubling of the practice," Carlo recalled. "I wanted to go to where I was getting all this information and see it for myself…I wanted to get my info-business off the ground and meet Dan." Carlo accessed resources that helped him implement faster and picked brains from top entrepreneurs.

Recalling his private two-day session with Dan Kennedy, Carlo said, "I got a handle on how to set up this business properly. I took Dan's advice and did not mess with it. I still refer to the notes, and although I've tried to break it several times…thinking, 'Maybe this way is better'…every time I do that, I've been met with the realization that if I just did what Dan said from the beginning, I get the results faster.

"The Magnetic Marketing System and Toolkit allowed me to really live life on my terms," Carlo reflected. "Previously, I was completely occupied and consumed with the business twenty-four seven and just not around. Even the time I was there, I was not present because I was preoccupied, thinking about ways to make the business better. It comes down to a lack of clarity and lack of certainty in the direction or in the execution that created that world. Now, it's totally different. My income has gone up another level, and I'm working far less. Now instead of having every minute of every day scheduled out for me, I can have the freedom to do what I want during the day. There are still things that need to get done, but I have the leverage of a great team. I have freedom of time, freedom of money to do as I wish. It wasn't immediate, but it definitely would not have changed, and I might not even be in dentistry at this point if I hadn't gotten involved in Magnetic Marketing and done something about it."

BUILDING YOUR MAGNETIC MARKETING® SYSTEM

CHAPTER 7

Your Magnetic Attraction System

What I'm going to describe to you over the next three chapters represents the foundational components of the complete Magnetic Marketing System. In over four decades, I've never met a single doctor who couldn't take this foundation and apply it for use in their practice.

When you put this system in place, you'll have a repeatable, reliable machine working for you 24/7/365 to attract-convert-retain patients. No more guesswork. No more "feast or famine." No more random acts of marketing.

In this chapter, we'll cover your Magnetic Attraction System—built to attract prospects who you know fit your targeted *WHO* and get them to raise their hand, indicating that they have a problem you can solve thanks to the healthcare services you have to offer.

The diagram below shows how the Attraction System works:

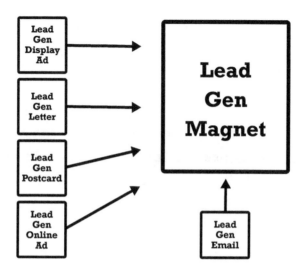

The Attraction System uses a variety of MEDIA channels where your target prospects hang out to let them know about your Lead-Generation Magnet.

These can include magazine ads, banner ads on websites, pay-per-click ads, emails sent to lists they've subscribed to, direct mail, business cards you hand out when meeting someone, display ads in newspapers, Valpak coupons, and so on.

The Lead-Generation Magnet is the special widget you are offering to get individuals—from the greater population of prospects—to indicate interest and thereby transform themselves from prospects into a "LEAD."

Once a lead raises their hand, you now have permission (and the responsibility) to follow up with them regarding the information they requested. For example:

➜ If they asked about dental implants and finally having a smile they can take pride in, you can follow up on this.

➜ If they asked about straightening their child's teeth, you can follow up with them on this.

➜ If they asked about problems with sleep apnea, you can follow up with them on this.

Everyone who raises their hand gets put into a "bucket" or database or list, from which you then follow up with messaging aimed at converting them from a Lead to a paying Patient.

This approach transforms your advertising from a "hope but can't tell if it works" model to a "know if it works" system. Now you're investing in reaching out directly to people you *KNOW* you can help and who have indicated they have a problem you can solve. You can run the numbers based on the results you're getting from your lead-generation ads—calculate to see that for every $1 you invest, you get $2–$4 or more back. This is a huge improvement over Goodyear blimp advertising, where there's no way to accurately measure and you have no idea whether the ads have any effect at all.

CREATING YOUR LEAD-GENERATION REPORT/ GUIDE/MAGNET

Typically, your Lead-Generation Magnet is information that has real value to the prospect.

It can be simple, brief, delivered via offline or online media, and crafted to attract exactly the patient you want.

> Your Lead-Generation Magnet is information that has real value to the prospect.

It can be a free report, or a checklist, or even a cheat sheet on a subject of prime interest to your preferred patient.

The purpose for all of these is to position you and your practice as reliable, knowledgeable experts in your field.

Your Lead-Generation Magnet has four main jobs:

1. First, to generate and enhance response to advertising.

2. Second, to reinforce and strengthen the prospect's unhappiness with the current circumstances and problems he has that you can provide the solution to.

3. Third, to establish both your expertise and empathy.

4. Fourth, to provide positioning so that the prospect is predisposed to accept your recommendations favorably.

In many cases, the free report is nothing more or less than a disguised long-copy persuasive sales letter, but if you called it that, no one would want it.

Instead, it's best to include legitimately valuable information. When you include such information, the prospect will see that you are a good source for answers to his problems, needs, and desires.

A lot of people balk at giving away valuable information, but that's a huge mistake. You give to get. If you don't reveal anything of value in your LGM, the prospect can assume there's no value in your products or services either.

Here are some examples of information-based Lead-Generation Magnets.

→ "How To Tell If Dental Implants Are Right For You." This report would lay out the benefits of dental implants, how they work, and why your practice has the expertise and know-how to provide the very best service possible.

→ "Six Keys to Getting a Great Night's Sleep." Obviously, one of the six ways would involve coming into your office for an exam to determine whether they have sleep apnea and possibly require treatment. The other five ways would be useful things the person can do on their own to get a good night's sleep.

→ "10 Ways to Make Sure Your Teen Has a Bright, Healthy Smile That Will Last a Lifetime." The report could include information on things like mouthguards for sports, proper dental hygiene including regular checkups, brushing, flossing, and the pros/cons of various teeth-straightening options—focusing on the one you provide.

HERE ARE A FEW IMPORTANT WRITING TIPS.

Avoid "Me, Me, Me, We, We, We" Speak

Some Lead-Generation Magnets talk too much about the practice and not enough about the prospect. He does not care about you, or your practice per se; he only cares about the wonderful things that will happen to him as a result of doing business with you. Translate every fact and feature listed in your report into a benefit. Be you-oriented, not me-oriented. Use all the data you gathered about your *WHO*, and talk to them in their language and about their real problems.

Don't Overeducate

You want to inform and impress, but not tell everything you know. Tell people what to do, but not how to do it. Let them take the next step to get the exact how-tos. In fact, one of the best responses you can get from your Lead-Generation Magnet is "Can you help me do this?"

Don't Forget the Call to Action

If you don't have a call to action (CTA), you've wasted your time and money. To paraphrase Zig Ziglar, "Is your free report a sales professional, or a professional visitor?"

> If you don't have a call to action (CTA), you've wasted your time and money.

Tell the prospect exactly what to do, when, why, and what will happen once he does. It's helpful to offer an immediate gratification incentive for that requested action, such as a special bonus or a discount. The CTA could be a number of things, depending on how complex your sales funnel needs to be.

→ You could go directly for the sale, including pricing, features, bonuses, guarantee, even a deadline.

→ You could offer some type of diagnostic consultation, with an invitation to set up an in-person call or face-to-face meeting.

→ Or you could send them to a website or some other additional information resource.

Create and Use Powerful Titles

The title of your Lead-Generation Magnet is very important. Like a headline, it has to interest people enough to want it, and then motivate them to consume it when they get it.

Take the time to create a really powerful title. Where do you get great titles? Model the attention-getting headlines you can find on supermarket tabloids, like *The Enquirer*, and on the covers of magazines like *Cosmopolitan*, *Reader's Digest*, and others.

These headlines have to sell those magazines off the rack. Of course, the subject matter probably won't fit dentistry, but the structures of these headlines will.

Making the Lead Gen Offer

Making the offer for the Lead-Generation Magnet involves two steps:

→ **Step 1: Sell the prospect on getting the Lead-Generation Magnet.**

→ **Step 2: Collect contact information for use in follow-up.**

(After you finish Step 2, you deliver the Lead-Generation Magnet, which leads right into the Conversion System, which I'll discuss in the next chapter.)

Let's talk about Step 1, which involves making a strong sales pitch to convince them to request the Lead-Generation Magnet.

Do NOT underestimate the difficulty in doing this, even though it's probably something you'll be giving away for FREE. People remain reluctant to share contact information, especially given the amount of unwanted spam they suspect will come their way, as well as privacy concerns.

So you need to very clearly make the case why your Lead-Generation Magnet will solve a specific problem, heal a burning pain point, or address a real heartfelt concern they're dealing with.

Your options for offering your Lead-Generation Magnet are many and varied:

→ Business card

→ Postcard

→ Phone script

→ Website

→ Facebook/YouTube/social media

→ Banner ad

→ Valpak insert

→ TV or radio commercial

→ Email

→ Speaking

You can (and should) offer your Lead-Generation Magnet anywhere and everywhere.

If you do so in person, it's easy; just get the prospect's business card or contact info. Then send them the Lead-Generation Magnet. Over the phone, just write it down. You can also drive people to an 800 number with a recorded message and have them leave their info there. While this may sound old school, it remains quite effective, especially when dealing with target markets that skew older.

Your Lead-Generation Magnet needs to sound sexy, exciting, informative—the magic pill to cure whatever ails you. The ad copy used to promote it likewise has to frame its benefits and value with powerful, emotional language. The Lead-Generation Magnet offers transformation, pure and simple, and anyone would be a fool not to take advantage of it and now.

One of the primary mechanisms today for collecting contact information is online with a dedicated, simple webpage called a landing page or squeeze page.

You probably already have a big, fat, catchall site that has a mountain of content on it.

If you're going to do lead generation, you should not send prospects into that. Instead, send them to a very simple landing page that works just like a clerk answering the phone.

The landing page, or squeeze page, is very, very simple. This is where you're going to capture the person's contact information who has come to your website from one of your lead-generation pieces.

The website is simple because the only reason they're coming to it is to give you their contact information in exchange for your Lead-Generation Magnet, so that's all you want to show them. It doesn't include any kind of navigation options or a menu bar with "Home," "About," etc., so they can't get lost someplace else on your website. The only purpose of this page is to collect contact information so you can send them your Lead-Generation Magnet and then follow up.

You're not trying to build a brand. Not trying to entertain or inform. You're not trying to get likes or anything like that—although those are not inherently bad. What you are trying to do, and what you want to measure, is to get the people who do show up to give you their contact information. That is the one and only goal of your landing page.

Once you have their information, you send them your Lead-Generation Magnet and then put them into your Magnetic Conversion System.

IT'S ALL ABOUT MAGNETIC ATTRACTION

This chapter should make 100 percent clear what I mean by Magnetically Attracting leads as opposed to chasing them.

Yes, you lay out the offer of a Lead-Generation Magnet—the free report, the information kit, DVD, audio, checklist, etc.—to everyone in your *WHO* that you can. But it's not chasing; it's simply laying it out there to see if anyone's interested enough to step out of the pack and raise their hand.

By doing so, you've enticed them to take that very first step on their own. They've crossed the first threshold barrier. It's a tiny step, to be sure, but it's an important one. They've said *YES* for the first time about something you have to offer.

Now it's up to you to build upon that momentum in your Magnetic Conversion System.

The Six Steps Dr. Tyler Williams Used To Quickly Accelerate His Dental Practice To 7 Figures

In 2015, Dr. Tyler Williams's practice was flatlining.

The two practices he'd purchased and merged together had been increasing 20 to 50 percent year after year. But after growing it to mid-six-figures from when he started in 2010, the practice not only plateaued, but total collections also dropped. "I thought if we added more people, we'll do better," Tyler said. "So we added two more team members, and all of a sudden, our numbers started slipping."

On top of that, he got hit with increased taxes. "The 4 percent drop with adding team members and then the increased taxes we had to pay really put me in a bind," Tyler recalled. "We'd just built a new house, and I got my wife, Megan, stressed out because I told her we'd have to take a whole bunch of money to pay taxes."

Depleting their savings to pay taxes lit a fire under Tyler. "I said, 'I'm never going to go through that again because it was just too stressful.'"

Hungry for answers, he took a $1 trial offer from Magnetic Marketing after hearing Dan Kennedy on a podcast. "What I realized is it wasn't the team members' fault," Tyler said. "It was my fault for not providing the tools to train them and hold them accountable."

Since joining Magnetic Marketing in 2016, Tyler doubled his practice, growing it to seven figures. He has eight employees, including a second full-time doctor. Planning for expansion, he's moving into a new building four times larger that he purchased. "That'll be a nice long-term investment for us where we can pay rent to ourselves and grow with the team," Tyler said.

He's found more time and location freedom too. For example,

he utilizes tele-dentistry, and 80 percent of what needs to get done can be handled by his team. If he hits his weekly goal early, he doesn't worry about taking Friday off.

> Profit and income are not directly related to time.

"There's nothing to sweat because we hit our numbers. Anything else is gravy," Tyler said. "It goes back to what Dan teaches us—that profit and income are not directly related to time."

Here's how Tyler accelerated his practice growth:

Step 1: Only Work With People Who Are A Good Fit

There are approximately 1,100 dentists practicing in the vicinity of Tyler's dental practice located in Murray, Utah, a suburb of Salt Lake City. While Tyler will take family members of patients, he primarily works with patients who fit his ideal patient avatar: an adult who requires comprehensive dental care, such as replacing old dental work, straightening teeth, or implants. His patients come from northern Utah as well as from surrounding states including Idaho, Wyoming, Nevada, and as far away as Anchorage, Alaska.

"Magnetic Marketing opened my eyes to the fact that for years, we catered our practice to the worst type of patients," Tyler said. "The ones who always complain about how much everything costs, cancel or 'no show,' or you have to see him a hundred times for follow-up. They fuss about everything that the good patients don't typically fuss about. Magnetic Marketing made it so much easier. Now we don't even hesitate for a second if someone's not a good fit; we quickly give them the option to be referred."

Today, he only markets to patients who fit his avatar and parts ways with patients that don't fit by sending a letter. "The letter explains that we want our patients to have the best care possible, and if we can't provide that at our location, here are some other options that may work better," Tyler explained. Providing them three recommendations, he includes a corporate-style practice and a practice that is cheaper but more hassle. "The reason we do that is a lot of times people get mad at the cost," Tyler said. "It helps people realize how great the service is at our practice after seeing the other practice. Occasionally, we'll get someone who will apologize profusely and come back a much better patient."

Step 2: Be More Visible

Expanding the types of media he uses, coupled with fast implementation, helped Tyler grow rapidly. He also applied Magnetic Marketing principles to existing marketing, such as his website. Media successes include the following:

Lumpy mail. "I started putting together sales letters and reactivation letters," Tyler recalled. "We started sending out lumpy mail not long after buying Dan's book. I went to the Dollar Store and bought a pack of plastic army men toys. I put them in letters and sent them to people who had untreated dental care with a headline that said, 'Your smile is under attack.' We got those going quickly. The ROI was mixed; however, I can tell you because of tracking, it was because we did a one-off-mailer. We didn't have a good follow-up system for that, yet I can still trace multiple patients back to that first mailer."

Street signs. Tyler creates and rotates inexpensive street signs, placing them along a road near his office. Each sign includes a headline, an offer, and a tracking number. "We get so much drive-by traffic that the return is incredible on this," Tyler said. "It even beats our listing on Google, where a lot of people find us. It's a good offline direct-response ad."

Step 3: Deepen Relationships

Tyler adapted personality-driven messaging in all his marketing after figuring out his newsletter wasn't as effective as it could be. At the time, he was using a company that created newsletters for dentists to send out to cold prospects. "That newsletter was OK," Tyler said. "It got a three-to-one response on the front end, and if you handle the first visit appropriately, the backend opportunity in dentistry can have a long-term source of income…but the problem was that most of the newsletter was just about dental procedures, and people don't really find that nearly as interesting."

Now Tyler and his team create a fun four-page newsletter themselves, which includes a personal story written by Tyler to help patients get to know him as a person. Newsletters are sent to three lists: 1) top prospects, 2) his patients, and 3) an internal newsletter to his team. "The patient newsletter is especially amazing at how well it helps you retain people," Tyler said. "People come in now and ask us, 'How's your daughter doing?' or 'I saw that you got stung by a stingray in Mexico.' People comment on these things and we know that it's working."

Tyler's found even more people are reading their mail, and the pass-along factor is even higher now that people are spending more time at home.

"They see we have a sense of humor," Tyler said. "It makes things fun. I kind of like to play on the cheesy dentist stereotype and tell cheesy dental jokes…people kind of laugh, but then they realize we're human and we care about them and that means more. It deepens the relationship."

Step 4: Develop Accountability

"The accountability of people, including myself, changed everything," Tyler said. He credits this for making better decisions, retaining good employees, making people feel involved and engaged, and removing stress by helping him know what to do. "I've appreciated what I've learned from Dan and the community as far as tracking and holding everyone accountable," Tyler said. "I've learned people will naturally weed themselves out if you hold them accountable. And I wasn't doing that very well five years ago. Developing a system of accountability helps people know where they stand at any given time. Magnetic Marketing helped shed a lot of light on how to do that and how to be equally accountable for everyone across the board."

> When a team member asks, "Should we do this?" I say, "This is great, but what do the numbers look like on it?" Cause if the math doesn't work, nothing else will work.

Every decision starts with the numbers. "Whatever marketing campaign we're doing, I'm looking at the ROI and who's responsible," Tyler said. "When a team member asks, 'Should we do this?' I say, 'This is great, but what do the numbers look like on it?' 'Cause if the math doesn't work, nothing else will work. That's made things a lot easier."

He even adapted an accountability system to allocate money in the business. A Magnetic Marketing Gold Call inspired his "Practice Profits Bucket System," which automates how much money should be transferred into each of his bank accounts for things such as taxes, payroll, future purchases, and operating expenses so he can plan ahead. "It just goes back to accountability," Tyler said. The system helps him to easily decide what to do with the extra money when he has a good month so he doesn't have to decide whether to cut himself a bigger check, prepay taxes, pay down loans, incentivize his team, and so on. "It takes the stress out because it removes indecisiveness," Tyler said. "You know exactly where everything needs to go."

Step 5: Create Momentum

Since 2018, Tyler has published three books and is close to finishing his fourth. He's also been featured on the radio and in other media outlets. His first two books are designed to attract his ideal patients, and his second two books are written to attract practice owners to his coaching business. "A book was something I always wanted to do," Tyler said. "Magnetic Marketing motivated me to get that done quicker and made it real. Having a book published really does build your credibility, but I wish I would have done it eight years ago. The momentum we could have built off that would have been much greater than it is now."

Step 6: Look For Windows Of Opportunity

When Tyler realized he didn't know how long the pandemic would slow his practice down, he capitalized on the extra time. Joining the Renegade Millionaire Virtual Coaching program, he launched his info-business, Pine Crest Dental Growth (Yourpracticegrowth. com), started a podcast (*The Practice X-Factor*), and wrote most of his fourth book during the two months when his practice was mostly shut down due to the COVID-19 pandemic. He also made videos and sent emails to his clients to stay connected. As a result, he had his best months ever in May and June 2020. "You have to look for those little windows of opportunity because you never know when they're going to pop up. You must be ready to pounce on it and make something happen.

"Since applying the Magnetic Marketing System and Toolkit to my business, I've realized that whenever there's a bottleneck or something is not working the way I want it to, it's easy to see the big picture and make adjustments. It helps you learn to see, 'Here's what I like to do and I'm good at...' and here's how to offload those things you're not good at. This gives you the time to focus more on what you want to do. Had I not joined the Magnetic Marketing community, our growth would have been much slower. Understanding and using these principles made all the difference from taking a path of single-digit growth to the path of double-digit growth that we're on now. It's like putting rocket fuel inside of your car. This really accelerated the process and helped give us much better focus and clarity."

CHAPTER 8

Your Magnetic Conversion System

Now that you have gotten your prospect to raise their hand, it's time to fire up your Magnetic Conversion System—the goal of which is to turn them from someone merely interested into a fully engaged patient.

The diagram below shows the different elements of the Conversion System:

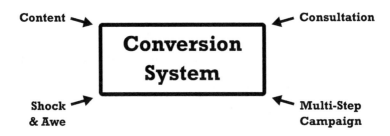

It's important to note that it's up to YOU to define exactly how to configure this system. The different components, each of which I'll describe on the following pages, can be mixed and matched and sequenced in different ways.

The key, however, is to implement _SOMETHING_. Far too many dental practices totally drop the ball when it comes to following up with leads who have already made it clear, either through action or communication, that they're interested in what you have to offer. It boggles the mind—you've paid good money for inventory, rent, power, licensing, website hosting, advertising, and more, yet you're willing to watch all that go down the drain by failing to follow up.

Indeed, this should inspire you because by putting this Conversion System in place in your practice, you will literally create an unfair advantage over your competition, who almost certainly won't do anything anywhere close to, or as detailed, or as systematic.

All the components of the system are based on one overriding principle:

"Show Up Like No One Else"

For just a second, let's go back to that question I said you should ask yourself when creating your Unique Selling Proposition (USP). Do you recall? It goes like this:

"Why should I choose you versus any and every other option of the same dental product or service that you provide?"

Such a powerful question, and you *HAVE* to be able to answer it in every communication you make with future and even current patients. Because as they say, every horse eventually goes lame—you can't simply assume that just because you've convinced someone to buy from you once they'll continue along that path forever. You constantly have to provide a good answer to that question throughout the entire patient life cycle.

> Every horse eventually goes lame—you can't simply assume that just because you've convinced someone to buy from you once they'll continue along that path forever.

Therefore, your goal in your Conversion System is to show up like nobody else. Stick out like a sore thumb among the tens of thousands of sales messages bombarding your prospects every day. And when you show up at the door—standing out from the semiwashed competitive masses—you arrive not only looking like something truly special, but you also bring heightened value that's clearly different.

It's important to understand that the higher up the income ladder you go, people will pay more for *WHO* you are rather than WHAT you do. The *WHAT* of what you do can easily be turned into a commodity. But *WHO* you are is unique—there's only one, and therefore the value is established accordingly.

Showing up like no one else reinforces that fact, which is why it must stay top of mind through all your communications as a Magnetic Marketer.

Let's talk about a few ways to do just that.

MULTISTEP CAMPAIGN

Most dentists' marketing is not very sophisticated at all. Here's what it looks like. Print up a brochure. A lot of them. Put them in a burlap sack. Rent a plane. Fly low. Shake a sack. Hope.

We can do better.

What we want to do is identify a small, carefully selected, manageable target market and set out to become the dominant presence in that target market in as short a period of time as possible.

Why small? The biggest marketing mistake most practices make is marketing too big. I'll ask, "What's your target market?" "Detroit." "Well, if we send one postcard to every adult who lives in the greater Detroit area once a year, which can hardly be called an intensive campaign, what's our budget got to be?" The guy says, "$300,000." "How much you got to spend?" "$600."

How's that going to work out?

Point being, you instead need to shrink the size of your target market to whatever resources you're willing and able to commit to allow you to have big impact. And here's the secret to that: if you want impact and you want response, then you must have repetition. They are inextricably linked. But you can't afford to do what Madison Avenue wants you to do—spend huge dollars on TV ads that play twenty-four seven—and maybe someday respond. That's not the answer.

> If you want impact and you want response, then you must have repetition. They are inextricably linked.

The answer is a series of communications—they could be letters, they could be emails, they could be postcards, they could be a blend—that take place over a short period of time, each one reiterating your offer and call to action.

There's magic in the multistep structure. I'd like to claim credit for its invention, but the truth of the matter is that I modeled it nearly fifty years ago. In one year, I managed to have two cars repossessed, and I went personally and corporately bankrupt. I got it all over in one year.

During that year I became intimately familiar with the collection industry, and I had a lot of time on my hands. I noticed a pattern, which I'll describe to you. It's first notice, second notice, third notice. They're typically fifteen days apart, although you don't have to adhere to that timing. Each one clearly refers to the previous one they sent you. We call that linkage. There's no mystery in that they're writing to you frequently. They get a little tougher as they go along. And the last one generally has copies of everything else they sent previously, rubber-stamped "Final Notice."

I said to myself, "If that will get money from people who haven't got any, offering them nothing, I wonder what would happen if we tried it on people who do have some and offered them something of value?"

This has turned out to be one of my most reliable Magnetic Marketing structures, which is why it has become the staple of my Magnetic Conversion System.

ADDING MORE CREDIBILITY WITH CONTENT

A simple three-step sequence works great for many products and markets. But there are times when you need to extend the sales timeline to increase your authority and credibility. In cases like these, you probably want to consider bolstering your positioning by following up on the initial Lead-Generation Magnet with additional related content.

This strategy is done quite often when launching a brand-new product or service. The initial Lead-Generation Magnet might be a video training, which is then followed up by a series of additional videos on that same topic. But you don't have to limit yourself to videos; you can follow up with any number of things, such as emails, reports, online assessments, even books.

When doing this kind of extended campaign, it's typical to hold off on asking for the sale up until the very end. Up to that point, you continue to provide valuable insights, and each new piece of content ends with a "stay tuned for coming attractions" message.

The final piece of content is where you would make your real call to action—laying out all the critical elements of your offer, features, benefits, pricing, guarantee, etc.

BLOWING THEM AWAY WITH "SHOCK AND AWE"

A related idea is to bundle a bunch of perceived "high-value" content items into a single package and then deliver them all at once in what's been called a "shock-and-awe" package.

The name is derived from the 1992 Gulf War, when US forces overwhelmed Saddam Hussein's military with overwhelming force. The objective with your marketing "Shock and Awe" is likewise to overwhelm the prospect with extreme evidence that you are indeed head and shoulders above any other dentist.

Your Shock-and-Awe package could include:

→ Consumer report guide(s): Reports written by you to position you as the expert that you are

→ CD/DVDs: Audio and/or video of interviews, guest appearances, podcasts, presentations, case studies, testimonials, etc. (anything showcasing authority and expertise)

→ Printed special report(s): Reports that are relevant to your message and/ or the prospects' challenges

→ Newsletters: Back copies of your monthly newsletter

→ Articles or press releases: Anything you have written or has been written about you

→ Self-Assessment and Score Analysis Tool

→ Testimonials: Anything and everything anyone has ever said about you, showing overwhelming proof that you are the only choice they should be going with

→ Lead-generation book (authored by you)

And don't limit your thinking to just serious information; you can include cookies, candy, toys, T-shirts, and so on. One previous client in the electronics industry sent, as a step in his conversion funnel, a briefcase with a video player built in, as well as a fresh king cake from New Orleans. A cover letter inside recommended that the prospect watch the video (which offered the service quite nicely) while enjoying a delicious piece of cake.

Now *THAT* made an impact. That is how you show up like nobody else.

You'll definitely want to include at least some item with your Call To Action, which could lead to either a direct sale or to an in-person meeting.

SELLING A CONSULTATION VERSUS A DIRECT-SALE OFFER

Most of what we've discussed so far in the Conversion System is based on the idea of using all these components to lead up to a direct sale for your product or service. The power of building this out into a sequential step-by-step process, with the Lead-Generation Magnet at the very beginning leading to one after the other, is that it creates a foundation for the prospect saying *"YES"* through an ongoing series of microagreements.

→ Prospect says *"YES"* to the Lead-Generation Magnet.

→ Then says YES to opening a follow up email and watching an online video.

→ Then says YES to taking an assessment sent in the mail.

→ Then says YES to reading a book sent to his home.

→ And so on and so on.

All these *YES* agreements build on one another, leading the prospect to feel more and more in agreement with what you have to say and offer. So when the final call to action appears, they have established the habit of saying *YES* to what you put before them. Of course, this doesn't guarantee the sale, but it absolutely makes it much more likely. People want to believe they behave with consistency. If you can get them to consistently say *YES*, you have started the ball rolling in the right direction.

Now in many specialties—for example, cosmetic dentistry—the actual sale can't be closed without first "selling" the prospect on agreeing to attend some kind of in-person consultation.

In these cases, you're using components of your Conversion System to lead directly to accepting that Consultation Meeting, and this could involve the multistep campaign, shock-and-awe box, ongoing content, etc.

The Consultation is where you, one-on-one, work with the prospect through their specific situation and craft the appropriate treatment plan to meet their needs. The Call To Action at the end would be to approve the treatment plan, sign the contract, the check, and close the deal.

If the deal does *NOT* close, you do *NOT* give up.

Instead, you continue moving forward with whatever components of the Conversion System you deem necessary, which again can include MORE content, MORE shock and awe, and MORE multistep campaigns of email/direct mail/postcards/etc.

How long should you keep this up?

As the old saying goes, "until they buy or die." Now, once someone does become a patient, we don't want our magnetic attraction to fade. For this reason, we continue with the Magnetic Retention System.

CHAPTER 9

Your Magnetic Retention System

This is the part of the puzzle that no one does. The part that can quickly and easily turn one patient into two, thus doubling the value of every new patient. And the best part is it's the easiest system to implement as part of the ongoing operations within your practice.

One of the most important keys to maximum patient value is in retention and repeat business. That is not something you're "entitled to" as a result of your excellent clinical care—although that doesn't hurt in the least.

Instead, it's a result of careful, strategic marketing, which includes continuing to market to them in a systematic way, not taking them for granted, and communicating again and again in a magnetically attractive manner.

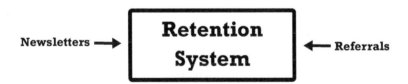

This requires frequently having and presenting a good answer to the question that is so important to us that it's become part of our vernacular. It's how we greet each other. That question is: *"What's new?"*

I don't say, "Tell me everything that's the same as it was the last time I saw you three months ago." I'm not interested in that. I'm interested in *"What's new?"*

If you don't have a good answer to "What's new?" they go looking for it somewhere else. A bored patient goes elsewhere. They forget about you. They don't talk about you. They don't buy from you, and they are easily wooed by some competitor who comes along with something that's new and exciting.

How do you answer this question that is always on their minds? And how do you do it consistently and repetitively, so they are always intrigued by you?

The answer to this question is by frequently and continually reinventing your practice inside your practice, by inventing new widgets and offering those new widgets through constant communication with your past and present patients.

At least once a month, if not more often, they are hearing from you, and they are getting a new widget offered to them. That will keep them interested and engaged, sell to them more frequently, and even get them to refer more often.

The point is, your complete Magnetic Marketing System should incorporate what, in direct-marketing lingo, is called "front end and back end."

→ *Front end* refers to outreach to attract and acquire new leads, new potential patients, and new patients.

→ *Back end* means developing and retaining those patients, increasing the frequency of repeat business you do with them, cross-selling different products and services, putting fresh offers in front of them frequently, and staying interesting to them so they stay with you and tell others about you.

How do you do that? There are two ways that are included in every Magnetic Retention System:

1. PATIENT NEWSLETTERS

Every dental practice should have some kind of patient newsletter that, at a minimum, hits their doorstep once a month. Preferably it would be a real, printed newsletter.

Why?

First off, it has a higher perceived value; a physical newsletter just looks like it has more value than an email. Secondly, it's more likely to get consumed. An email—maybe it'll get opened, maybe not. But if you get something in the mail that you have to open up and look at, and it's at least minimally fun and interesting, then it's far more likely to get read and possibly even retained.

And that brings up the third reason a real-life, honest-to-gosh print newsletter has value: if they keep it around, it lingers as an ongoing reminder of your existence. You're no longer a memory of some service once rendered. You're there in the file cabinet letting me know that you cared enough to make the effort to send me something new rather than discard all memory of me to the dustbin of history.

Your monthly patient newsletter should include:

 → Content that reaffirms your uniqueness (remember that USP?) and authority in your practice's area of expertise. But keep this minimal, as little as absolutely necessary. (For heaven's sake, do *NOT* make your entire newsletter about dentistry. Nobody wants to hear about "the use of guided bone regeneration" from their local dentist.) Instead, you want to continue the conversation that you know they are having in their heads—continue to talk about problems you know that they have. For instance, everyone is interested in better health and looking better; these topics are universally on everyone's mind.

→ Content that's fun for the sake of being fun—puzzles, brainteasers, jokes, recipes, cartoons, funny memes, lighthearted fodder that offers some entertainment value. You want your patients to look forward to this every month. Puzzles and brainteasers are also what we call *engagement devices*, meaning that your newsletter will have staying power while they are engaged with it.

→ In line with "What's new?" some kind of call to action for your latest widget. You are in business after all, and you want to constantly remind patients that you offer valuable resources and services that will make their lives better. This is a great place to offer your newest consumer report or special report on a newsworthy topic that is plaguing them.

→ And finally, personality. When you create a bond with your patients, they are less likely to choose another provider over you, because you have become a friend. Your newsletter allows you to continue your relationships. By telling stories and sharing what is happening in your life, you let your patients bond with you.

→ And one of the best reasons for doing all you can to retain patients is to get them to refer you to their friends, family, and colleagues.

2. REFERRALS / WORD OF MOUTH

Word-of-mouth marketing is the most powerful and beneficial kind of advertising or marketing that you could ever have for a practice for the very simple reason that what others say about you is ten times more believable than what you say about yourself.

Way back when Anaheim, California was still a swamp,

> Word-of-mouth marketing is the most powerful and beneficial kind of advertising or marketing that you could ever have for a practice for the very simple reason that what others say about you is ten times more believable than what you say about yourself.

Walt Disney wrote a marketing principle that was taught to everybody involved with Disney, and it is a wonderful principle. It says:

"The way to be very successful in marketing is to do what you do so well that people can't resist telling others about you."

So one of the things you have to be continually asking yourself about your own practice is: "How can we do what it is that we do here so well that people can't resist telling others about us?"

For example, when a patient comes in the door, we teach the staff not to sit behind the desk and kind of look up at them and grunt and hand them paperwork to fill out. Instead, our staff should stand up, come out from around the counter, shake the patient's hand, and say, "Hi, Mr. Patient, welcome to X, Y, Z Clinic" or "Hi, Mr. Patient, good to see you today. How are you feeling?"

Then walk that patient through a greeting process unlike any other doctor's office he's ever gone to—in fact, it's unlike how he's treated anywhere else he goes to.

And a lot of those little things added together now result in what we call the wow experience. This person leaves your office and thinks to himself: "Wow, I've got to tell somebody. This is the most interesting, amazing, best thing that's happened to me all day!" (This relates to the "Show up like no one else" principle, but it's embraced throughout your entire practice, not just during conversion.)

And when you can create that for your patients, you know when they leave your place of business saying, "Gee, I was feeling kind of down when I came in here, but this is the best thing that's happened to me all day. This is just wonderful."

And they run into their next-door neighbor when they're now at home, and they're going to tell that guy about you.

If you do that, they're going to spread the word without you even having to ask, and that has immense power.

When we earn this level of enthusiasm from our patients—by blowing them away with service, quality, the whole shebang, way beyond what they ever expected—we do indeed earn the right to ask. And it's amazing to me how many dentists just never in any way, shape, or form, ask their patients for referrals.

I grew up in direct sales, selling in the home, face-to-face with moms and dads. I was taught and beat over the head with a very simple mechanism: as soon as you made that sale, you put a card or a form and a pen in front of your customer, and you said something to the effect of: "You know, most of my customers come to me as referrals from satisfied customers like you. And I'll bet you know five or six people who probably live right here in the neighborhood who would love to have whatever it was that I was selling just like you got. And I would be eternally grateful if you would let me use your name when I gave them a call to set up an appointment. And if you would take time right now to get your Christmas card book out or, you know, your personal phone book and just give me those five names and addresses, I'd really appreciate it."

And nine times out of ten, I'd walk out of that house maybe not with five, but with three or four good, solid names, addresses, and telephone numbers, and most of them would turn into appointments, and some of them would turn into sales.

Now, I learned that discipline when I was a pup, and I am always amazed at how many people don't use it. Every dentist should be asking for referrals.

When do you ask for referrals? Right after you've done something praiseworthy for your patient. Like when they see the results of the in-office teeth whitening and say: "Wow, this looks better than I ever expected!"

That's the time for you to say something like: "Hey, you know, we're trying to grow the practice here. We're taking on some new equipment, and you know we really depend on patients like you for referrals. I wonder if you would just take a few of your business cards and jot down on the back of each one the name and the phone numbers of a few people that I can call and talk to."

And when you ask, you get.

Here's perfect proof of this. One of the most challenging groups I've found to convince to do referrals are chiropractors; for some reason they seemed to have a hang-up about this. Even so…we devised a plan.

They offered a back-care class in their clinic that all the patients come to in a group and then they teach them about their back and how to take care of themselves. We came up with a very simple mechanism where at the end of the class the doctor essentially says: "Oh, by the way, many of you got here as a result of being referred by somebody who cared enough about you to refer you, and that's how we get most of our new patients. We would really appreciate it if you would refer others too. And for that reason I am passing out these forms."

They passed out these little forms that had places for ten names, addresses, and telephone numbers. And they asked them to fill them out and said they're going to send them some introductory information about chiropractic.

Now, they did that very fast, and it's a very soft request. It is very painless. It's done at the end of the class, so if somebody doesn't want to do it, it is easy for them to just leave the form on their chair and sneak out of the office.

Guess what happens? Seven out of ten patients fill out the form and turn in the form with somewhere between three and ten names and addresses and telephone numbers. It costs nothing to get those names, addresses, and telephone numbers.

Of course, then those names, addresses, and telephone numbers get plugged into the three-step campaign system, and one-third of them become new patients.

All from the power of simply asking for referrals.

Do You Own A Practice Or Are You Self-Employed?

How Dr. David Phelps created MORE time and a better, multimillion-dollar business, working less

In 2004, Dr. David Phelps needed freedom, *FAST*.

His only child, Jenna, aged twelve, was in end-stage liver failure and needed a lifesaving liver transplant.

David owned a dental practice and invested in real estate on the side. And although his practice was successful, he didn't really have a business. "It was a job," David explained. "A well-paying job, but let's be clear. There is a difference between being in business and being self-employed. I was self-employed, and that comes with the benefit of trading time for dollars at a relatively high level, but there's no real freedom."

David tried to sell his practice to bring in the extra cash they needed, but things didn't work out, and the sale to another dentist fell through—and the process resulted in the practice being in rough shape. Half his employees were gone, and the top tier of his patient base had moved on. "I was in a smaller community," David said. "That was good when things were good, and I wanted to make a name for myself. But it's bad if there's anything negative. So I had to overcome that."

David faced a tough decision—either put the scrubs back on and be the dentist again, taking the next two to four years to bring his practice back up and then sell again with a different plan. Or he could just shut down the practice and sell off the depreciated equipment and call it a day.

He didn't like either option. "Neither one felt good," he said.

"I didn't want to go back and be the dentist because I had mentally exited. But I also didn't want to just shut down something that I had built over many years. I had a reputation, and I felt like I still had people that relied on me."

Within the year, David found Magnetic Marketing after reading Dan Kennedy's book *No B.S. Time Management for Entrepreneurs.* "I thought, 'This guy is speaking to me,'" David said. "He's talking about all the issues that I feel as the solopreneur in this practice."

Signing up as a Gold Member, David began applying what he was learning from Magnetic Marketing. First, he addressed his mindset, changing from being the technician to creating a business that wasn't always dependent on him. He brought on associate dentists and new staff and expanded the hours of his practice.

And the biggest piece—he didn't go back to being a clinician. Instead, he became the marketer of his practice. He did PR, formed strategic alliances, and sent out direct mail and newsletters. Three years later, in 2010, David finally did sell his practice successfully and in the low seven figures. "The only reason it happened is because I had a real business that wasn't dependent on me," David said.

A Key Lesson From David's Setback

"I learned a lot from my setback," David said. "The adversity we go through in life, if we persist and carry it through, often leads to new revelations that we either never knew about or never thought were possible. Today, I don't worry about things I can't control. I just know there's always a pathway to the next thing. The final exit of my practice taught me something I never thought was true. I thought as a doctor, you had to be the doctor, and no one else would accept anything less. And that's not necessarily true."

Campaigns That Turned the Dental Practice's Business Around

Because patients were lost during the turmoil and upheaval from the first unsuccessful sale, David's inaugural campaign was a reactivation campaign to win past patients back. David followed Dan's advice to be transparent and give a real reason why they should come back. He showed vulnerability but took ownership. "I explained that I sold the practice to somebody who I thought was going to be good," David said. "I wrote, 'It didn't work out. It's on me. So I'm back, and here's what I'm doing.'"

David also did community outreach and asked patients for referrals. He advertised that he now had three doctors and was expanding hours, so he was seeking new patients. He let the community know they could expect improved service, a better customer service experience, and more access to his practice. Following Magnetic Marketing principles, he redid his website, setting up lead capture devices so he could collect contact information and start building a list. David used newsletter inserts, direct mail (he found oversized postcards particularly effective), and multistep campaigns. "Don't just do a one and done," David said. "Do a succession of touchpoints like we are taught through Magnetic Marketing."

Don't Sell; Do THIS Instead

David changed from selling to building relationships. "Don't just try to sell somebody to come in and become a patient on day one," David said. "Because that's only a small percentage of people that are ready to take action that day. I started to actually build a list, which I'd never done before."

David segments his lists, uses different media, and builds relationships by speaking to different segments with messages relevant to them at different times along the pathway. "The media platform becomes crucial," David said. "You'll only get that by starting somewhere, getting a message out and getting feedback to see who you resonate with…but you've got to know your tribe. You want your avatar to say, 'He or she knows me better than I know myself. He knows how I feel…my challenges. He can articulate it better than I can.' When you get to that point, you're on to something."

Sometimes LESS Is More

Rather than going crazy on adding more and more marketing, David focused on getting better. He got better at copywriting. Better at messaging to his avatar. He attributes being able to do this to measuring response rate and ROI on his marketing. "Measuring response rate actually became fun for me," David said. "I never really understood how much that could affect the business if it's done well." Through measuring and testing, he was able to orchestrate, be better, or provide better messaging. "Don't worry if it's going to work; just test it," David recommends.

David didn't overcomplicate things. He followed the advice he was being given through Magnetic Marketing "The fundamental and basic is what works," David added. "You can always add to that, but you don't have to go crazy and do SEO and a bunch of frills or turn to bright, shiny objects when you need to turn things around. Just start with the basics and then add to it."

> You don't have to go crazy and do SEO and a bunch of frills or turn to bright, shiny objects when you need to turn things around. Just start with the basics and then add to it.

Where to Get Good Ideas and Inspiration

In his forties when he finally sold his practice, David began to think about what to do next. "I thought about what I knew," David said. "This became my information marketing business that came out of the ashes of what was my practice sale." He combined his firsthand knowledge of the struggles doctors and dentists have with his knowledge and experience in real estate and created a Mastermind Group, inviting the doctors and dentists who wanted to learn how to do what he'd done.

David credits attending his first Magnetic Marketing Summit in 2009 with coming up with this idea. "I started getting engaged and saw a different world," David said. "I thought, 'Wow, this is something that's kind of fun.' I started to get a little bit of a feeling of how it might work. So ten years later, I have Freedom Founders. And I have to say it's probably the most fun I've had my whole life."

David added, "Where we get inspiration and where we get clarity on ideas and what opportunities there are is by being around other people that are entrepreneurial, who can see things that we can't see…if you are in a group of other people who also have experience in life through the same kind of challenges, different industry, different businesses, but can help us see different ideas…*that* gives you clarity. And clarity is what gives us the confidence to step forward into something new. So I have to say that without the Magnetic Marketing community, there's no telling what I'd be doing. I don't think I'd be doing what I do today, which is what I love. I love the people I get to work with every day. I don't even care what day of the week it is on a calendar. Every day is the same in terms of vibrancy and purpose and enjoying what I get to do."

Invest in Yourself

Starting from zero, David has built his info-business, Freedom-Founders.com, to a multimillion-dollar company with a 40 percent profit margin. To scale his business and speed things up, David credits investing in training. "I'm investing heavily," David said. "I'm in Masterminds. I'm a Magnetic Marketing Diamond Member. I moved to Titanium with Dan Kennedy. I'm putting money out because I have this passion, and I've found I can help people. So I want to know how I can do this on a bigger scale? Investing gives you speed because it gives you clarity, so you get traction quickly."

And as for David's daughter? She is doing well too. The last nine years have been the best years of her life in terms of health, which has given her a chance to catch back up. Attending community college, she wants to go into occupational or physical therapy. "She missed so much school the first eighteen years of her life, being in and out of hospitals," David explained. "She's making great strides now, and it's a blessing. She couldn't even read or write beyond maybe second grade at age sixteen. That's how chemo, the drugs, the missing school affected her. There are so many challenges, and it's just amazing to see how the brain can recover. Now she has more of a normal life, and she's going forward."

CHAPTER 10

Applying the Magnetic Marketing® Systems

I want to share with you a story that illustrates how any dentist could take everything we've discussed so far and put it into their own Magnetic Marketing System. It's really important that you go through it carefully. Here's why:

→ First of all, it takes everything we talked about so far and a few things we didn't, and stitches them together in chronological application order so you see how they work.

→ Secondly, it does it in a practical, true-life example.

→ Third, it does it for a regular general practice dentist, typically not known for good marketing, thereby demonstrating if this guy can do it, you can do it too.

→ Fourth, it gives you a complete marketing strategy, a system, step-by-step, that you can use exactly as it is described to you in this story and see results in your bank account in twenty-one days or less.

→ And there's a bonus. It gives you a new market, a farm, a group of prospects perfect

> for you, which you already have access
> to but are not currently harvesting.

For it to do all of those things, every little nuance is important; you will want to pay close attention.

One day, in the mail, I got an envelope. The envelope is addressed to me, Mr. Dan Kennedy. It has a real, live stamp on it. And in the return address corner is the name of someone I know, a colleague in business who also lived in my hometown.

> The takeaway for you is the envelope is from someone whose name I recognize. It's addressed to me. And it's got a real postage stamp on it. Not "bulk rate"—a stamp. What I've just described to you is one almost certain way to get an envelope opened. It's not the only way. Sometimes it's not the best way in a given situation, but it is a very good way.

So I opened it. The letter headline across the top of the letter says, "I suppose you're wondering why I'm writing to you about a dentist." I say to myself, "Yup. What's this all about?"

> Second takeaway. If you want to make your marketing work, write down, "Got to get them to open it; got to get them to read it." And you've got about ten seconds from flap to trash to compel readership. Curiosity is one way to do it. Not necessarily the best, but it's the way that was used here. (By the way, it's exactly the same with email. You need to have a great subject line if you want people to open and read your emails.)

The letter goes on to tell a story about how my colleague was having a party at his home on a Friday evening to which I had not been invited, and at about nine o'clock at night, while heading down the stairs to reinforce party supplies, he slipped and fell. In the fall, his mouth struck the railing just right to knock out a tooth.

There was blood, pain. It was a mess.

He did manage to recover the tooth and then tried to find a dentist who would be open to help him in this emergency; his regular dentist had just retired, and he had not transitioned to a new one at that time. He did a quick search on his smartphone and found this guy, Al the dentist, who agreed to open up his practice right then and there. A quick trip into town and before you know it, Al was able to save the tooth and the situation.

And in order to say thank you to this dentist for this extraordinary service, he decided to send this letter to all of us, his colleagues who live in town, and let us all know that if we ever need a dentist, Al's the guy we've got to call.

There's more you have to know about the Al story. But a major money-making thing just happened. It's called a *champion circle of influence*. Everybody has a circle of influence in which you could do business if you were properly introduced, but you haven't been.

The dentist goes back to the customer and says, "You know, when you came in the other night, you were very grateful, and I appreciate that. What you probably don't know is we get very few of our new patients the way we got you, from SEO and searches. We get most of our new patients through people like you, because you probably belong to something. You belong to Rotary?"

"No."

"Country club?"

"No."

"Homeowners' association?"

"No."

"Well, everybody belongs to something."

The guy confesses. He says, "Well, there is this speakers' association I belong to."

"Great! How many of those are there in Phoenix?"

"Three hundred."

Here's the second thing. The dentist says, "Here's what I'd like to do. I wrote up what you said to me as I left, now as a letter from you to those three hundred people. We can change anything you want to change. But then I want to take it, and I want to put it on your stationery. Again, not mine, yours. I want to put it in your envelopes. Not mine, yours. And I want to send it to those three hundred people who know you by name but do not yet know me. I pay for everything. May I do that?"

> That's called an endorsed mailing to a champion circle of influence. It's the only piece of mail on the planet where 100 percent get opened and 100 percent get read.

So I got the envelope, opened the envelope, and read the whole letter.

And when I got all done with it, I didn't call Al the dentist.

Why didn't I call Al the dentist? Right, because I didn't need a dentist. Sure. So all that's wasted, isn't it?

Wrong.

If he stops there, it's a giant, epic waste.

Think of what has to happen now for it to turn into business for the dentist. I got the letter and read it. Al sounds like a pretty good guy. But I don't need a dentist, at least not now. I'm in between dentists like my friend, but I'm in no hurry to go through the hassle of finding one.

But for this to work for Al, I'd have to make a dozen copies of this letter, then get a dozen ziplock sandwich bags and a dozen pieces of duct tape, and I'd have to put a letter in each bag, then I'd have to go around and stick one in the dozen or so places I walk by every day at my home and office—on the fridge, by my bed, in my car, etc., so someday when I decide I *DO* need a dentist, I can find this guy.

This is no way to get a flood of business.

That's why, about ten days later, I got what I would call letter number one from Al the dentist.

"Hi, I'm Al the dentist. You remember me? I'm the guy your friend wrote to you about, who had the party you weren't invited to, who had the dental emergency I rushed out and took care of. Now the reason I'm writing to you now is we have this very important free thing we do only for people referred to us from our VIP customers. That free thing is a free comprehensive oral healthcare audit. And the reason why it's so important for you to have a free comprehensive oral healthcare audit is every adult forty-five years old or older who doesn't have a regular dentist has at least twenty-seven horrible oral health conditions that could flare up and cause massive problems at a moment's notice. And all you have to do is swing by my office and we'll make sure none of those things are about to happen to you, for free."

> Notice what Al's just done. He's using his "Free Comprehensive Oral Healthcare Audit" as a Lead Gen Magnet to get me to raise my hand and invite him to provide further information. Yes, it's a consultation, but because he's already established credibility through the endorsed mailing from my buddy, the threshold barrier's been lowered enough to go with this as a first step. Of course, Al could've offered instead a more standard LGM like a report, "Twenty-Seven Horrible Oral Health Nightmares and How to Prevent Them—Guaranteed!" in his system. Again, in this, the audit works just fine.

I still don't call Al the dentist.

Now I'm starting to feel some dull throbbing in my jaw late at night that I wasn't noticing before, but I still don't call Al.

That's why ten days later, Al the dentist, sends me a second notice.

"Hi, I'm Al the dentist. You remember me? I'm the guy your friend wrote to you about, had the party you weren't invited to, lost the tooth. I wrote to you about our free comprehensive oral healthcare audit. I haven't heard from you, and I'm very concerned. If you'll take a look at the enclosed article reprint, you'll see why."

And I take this article reprint out of the envelope. It's from a small community newspaper. Everybody knows everybody. They only publish once a week. Here's a front-page story about an elderly man who, after years of nudging by his kids, finally visits the dentist. When he gets checked out, the dentist discovers a seed stuck in the gums—with a tiny plant actually starting to grow. And that wasn't the worst of it; after cleaning all the plaque, it was clear that the gunk was the only thing holding several of his teeth in place. There's a photo of the man smiling but without any front teeth.

I go back to the letter, and it reads,

"As you can see, even small oral health problems can become big oral health problems when ignored or left to themselves."

I still don't call Al the dentist.

But now I'm looking in the mirror a little closer and thinking, "I don't see anything that looks leafy to me."

Ten days later, Al the dentist sends his third "final notice" letter:

"Dan, we've twice offered you our free comprehensive oral healthcare audit. We haven't heard from you, but we sure have heard from a whole lot of other smart folks. That's why if you want the free comprehensive oral healthcare audit, it's very important you call within the next seventy-two hours. Otherwise, we may have to put you on a waiting list of up to one hundred days. And enclosed is a list of some of the oral health and dental problems that may occur during…"

I call Al the dentist.

Now, I'm going to tell you the rest of the Al story in a second, but first let's do some quick analysis. Al the dentist did everything we've talked about brilliantly. Let's analyze his marketing campaign.

Al the dentist, our marketing genius, goes and he gets himself a small, carefully selected, manageable target market. His is his *champions circle of influence*, one of the most productive farms you'll ever own.

The first seed he plants in his farm is the endorsed mailing, the only piece of mail that 100 percent gets delivered, 100 percent gets opened, 100 percent gets read.

He then kicks off his campaign with a sequence of communications.

> He creates a Lead-Generation Magnet, which is the offer of a free oral healthcare audit.
>
> He continues to pound this offer, referencing prior mailings, adding urgency with a final notice.
>
> He did everything we talked about brilliantly.
>
> And if he can do it, you can do it too.
>
> Now let's talk about showing up like no one else.

A week before my appointment, a package arrives by FedEx. There's a letter describing the upcoming visit and what to expect. There's several issues of Al's patient newsletter. A book by Al entitled, *How to Have a Smile That Lights Up Every Room You Enter*, packed with tips on oral health and stories from happy patients.

The day before the appointment, I get a text message and an actual phone call reminder, making sure to let me know how much they're looking forward to meeting me and how important my dental health is.

When I arrive at Al's dental office, I discover no resemblance to what I expect when I think "dentist." There's nothing that looks or gives off any hint of antiseptic or cold. It's warm, inviting, reassuring. The air is filled with the aroma of freshly baked cookies sitting on a table. Classical piano music is piped in.

The nice lady at the front desk doesn't wait for me; she comes out to greet me with a smile and pleasant welcome. The necessary paperwork takes but a minute to complete, as much of it was filled in already. As I sit, a video plays on a TV screen detailing stories of several patients—including my friend, who nearly lost a tooth but fortunately now has an even better smile, thanks to Al's exclusive teeth-whitening solution…now available for a limited time at a very special price.

About the time I finish my paperwork, the video ends, and the nice lady escorts me to the treatment room, where she introduces me to the dental assistant who'll be helping Al with my "exam."

The chair is comfortable, with relaxing music; everything's calm and reassuring. After a moment, Al arrives, smiling, warm, and professional. He conducts his exam and takes photographs explaining every step along the way.

I'm comfortable and relaxed throughout the entire process, which takes precisely the amount of time promised earlier.

"Mr. Kennedy, I have very good news for you. You do not have twenty-five of the twenty-seven most common oral healthcare problems. The ones you do have are very trivial. Let me show you."

Al goes through the photographs and shows me exactly what needs to be done; there's an old filling that needs replacing and some other minor preventative work. He explains everything clearly without a hint of judgment. He's totally friendly and professional.

"We can schedule them for a future appointment. For now, I recommend a basic cleaning, as it's been a while. We can take care of that today. Also, did you happen to see the video talking about our current special on whitening?"

Yep, I watched it.

"While you're here today, shall we just take care of the hygiene, or shall we make sure you walk out with a fresh, brighter new smile as well?"

A little later, I leave Al's office with that brighter smile, appointment set (and prepaid) for my other issues, and I drive away.

I was intrigued, so I called him a few days later. "Look, I didn't want to bother you when I was at your office. I know that's rude. But

I teach Magnetic Marketing Systems, and you used one of them brilliantly. I wonder if you'd mind sharing the numbers?"

Al says, "Not at all. I'll just have to put you on hold and get your file."

I'm now on hold, listening to a recorded commercial for his brother's financial planning service. When that's over, he's back.

"What would you like to know?"

"How many homes did you mail to?"

"About three hundred."

"How many of those oral healthcare audit things have you done so far?"

"Seventy-two."

At an average annual patient value of approximately $800 at least, do the math, if you wish. Assume no one but me gave him any money immediately. A poor assumption on your part, but make it if you wish.

For the price of three hundred letters times three, he's had seventy-two patient visits, where both in person, through his team, and via preappointment packages, he's put on a show and a half.

When they need a dentist, who are they going to call?

Of course Al's patient newsletter, *Keep On Smiling*, arrives within the week.

Again…who are they going to call?

You get the picture.

THAT is how you work the Magnetic Marketing System, soup to nuts. And if a typical dental practice could do it, it's a pretty sure bet your practice can do so as well.

NOW IT'S
UP TO YOU

When you come to a fork
in the road, take it.

—Yogi Berra

There are three steps to positive change:

1.   Awareness

2.   Decision

3.   Action

With this book, I have provided *Awareness.* There is a better, more productive, more differentiated approach to growing a practice by applied attraction rather than by pursuit; by focused targeted marketing rather than mud-against-wall and hope; and by an organized system rather than random and erratic acts.

Now you face a *Decision* **that is entirely yours to make.** The legendary attorney Gerry Spence almost always closed his ending speech to juries by telling an old, old parable about the wise man and the smart-aleck boy. The wise elder made himself available every Saturday for the villagers to line up and ask for his advice. The boy resented his authority and developed a plan to humiliate "Mr. Know-It-All." The boy captured a small bird and concealed it in his hands and stood before the wise man and asked if the bird in his hands was alive. Or was it dead? If the wise man said "Alive," the boy intended to quickly crush it to death and let it fall to the ground. If the wise man said "Dead," the boy would open his hands and let it fly free. But the wise man proved truly wise with his answer: "Son, that bird is in *your* hands."

Whether you end with having read this book, nodded in places, wished you could remake your practice to be "magnetic" but default to continuing to conduct business just as you do now and as your competitors do—*or* you take the next steps to a road less traveled with great potential—is entirely in *your* hands. Frankly, the person who reads but does act is no better off than the illiterate dunce who cannot read. The person who endlessly procrastinates and excuses himself from decisive action is no better than the somnambulant sloth.

The road to the ruin is paved with good intentions. And, as an old saying goes, "If wishes were horses, every man afoot would ride." Creative, constructive Action is what actually brings about positive change.

There is good news about Action. Business today is complicated. It is easy to feel overwhelmed. Are you too busy just making a living to make any real money? Or a better life? That is understandable but should be unacceptable. So that is where the organization built around the Magnetic Marketing System can step in, step up, and work right alongside you in implementing a series of dramatic breakthroughs. Those next steps are offered on the very next page.

You can soon own a fully functional practice and profit-building SYSTEM of your own…or you can continue as you are.

That bird is in *your* hands.

Visit us online to access these valuable resources.

Where Should I Start?

The most common question we get from Dan Kennedy book readers and entrepreneurs who find us after hearing about Magnetic Marketing is…"Where Should I Start?" Dan Kennedy has been at this for over 40 years and has a vault of content that's the size of a small bank, not the vault in a bank, but enough content to fill a small bank. The quick two question survey will provide you a simple road map to success **whether you're finding us for the first time, or you are an advanced student** of Magnetic Marketing and Dan Kennedy.

➜ Get Started at
  MagneticMarketing.com/get-started-dental

How Magnetic is Your Marketing Today?

One reason so many practice owners become advertising victims is because they don't understand the foundation of the Magnetic Marketing system. **For a limited time, we're offering a complimentary "How Magnetic Is Your Business & Your Marketing Assessment" to listeners and readers of Magnetic Marketing.** Record your answers to 8 short questions to find out how magnetically attractive you currently are. Your answers will unlock access to your personalized roadmap for your practice.

➜ Complete your Assessment at **MagneticMarketing. com/magnetic-practice**

60-Day Test Drive of Magnetic Marketing Gold Membership

Get **Instant Access** to Dan Kennedy's Magnetic Marketing System (what this entire book is about!) and **A 60 Day Trial** of the No B.S. Magnetic Marketing Newsletter for just 2 easy payments of just $59.97. Plus, if you take us up on this VERY Special, Limited Time

Offer, you'll also receive **6 Gifts Valued At $950.85**…and even if you decide to leave our community after 60 Days, you'll keep these bonuses as our gift to you.

→ Start Your Test Drive Today at **MagneticMarketing. com/book-test-drive**

Magnetic Marketing in Action

On the Magnetic Marketing Podcast, each week we bring on members of the Magnetic Marketing community who are implementing Magnetic Marketing in their businesses and practices. Learn from the best as they share what's working, what's not working, what they have learned, and what is fueling their growth today.

→ Listen to the Latest Episodes at
MagneticMarketing.com/podcast-reader

Take the Patient Relationship Assessment

Find out your Patient Relationship Score today!
During times of uncertainty there is ONE thing that can help your practice prosper and provide you with the stability and opportunity to grow your practice as you desire.

What is It?
A High Patient Relationship Score. There's no better way to ensure your success than to create lifelong relationships with your existing patients.

We've created a simple 9 Question Assessment that will reveal your Patient Relationship Score in under 3 minutes and share with you exactly how you can quickly improve your score.

→ Get Your Patient Relationship Score Now at
mLiveSoftware.com/assessment

CPSIA information can be obtained
at www.ICGtesting.com
Printed in the USA
JSHW012010090123
35995JS00008B/487

9 781950 863693